The Welfare State in Britain

The Welfare State in Britain

A Political History since 1945

MICHAEL HILL

Professor of Social Policy
University of Newcastle upon Tyne

Edward Elgar

Published by
Edward Elgar Publishing Limited
Gower House
Croft Road
Aldershot
Hants GU11 3HR
England

Edward Elgar Publishing Company
Old Post Road
Brookfield
Vermont 05036
USA

A CIP catalogue record is available from the British Library

Library of Congress Cataloging-in-Publication Data
Hill, Michael J. (Michael James), 1937–
    The welfare state in Britain : a political history since 1945/
Michael Hill.
        p. cm.
    Includes bibliographical references and index.
    1. Great Britain—Social policy—History—20th century. 2. Great
Britain—Politics and government—1945– 3. Welfare state.
    I. Title.
 HV248.H55   1993
 361.6'5'0941—dc20   92–42191
                                                         CIP

ISBN 1 85278 436 9
     1 85278 437 7 (Paperback)

Printed in Great Britain at the University Press, Cambridge

Contents

Tables

Preface

The Beveridge Report was published in 1942, and the National Health Service was established in 1948. Typically social policy histories concentrate upon the events which occurred before these crucial dates in the development of the ish welfare state. Changes since those dates, and particularly the changes of the 1980s, have made it necessary to recognise that the modern shape of social policy owes as much to events in the period of about 50 years since the 1940s as it does to events before the 1940s. This book therefore deals with the post-1945 period and may be considered to be a post-welfare state history.

The approach of the book is to concentrate upon the political events of the period, with the divisions between chapters determined by the changes in power at Westminster. The book will be concerned to explain the political events of the period which had an impact upon British social policy. In doing so it will examine the notion that there was a political consensus on social policy, particularly in the early part of the period. Another theme to be given attention is the idea that a crisis for the welfare state developed in the 1970s. In relation to this the extent to which the agenda for social policy was radically altered by the Thatcher governments will be examined.

From 1979 until the time of writing there has been continuous Conservative rule. A decision had to be taken on where to end the narrative. What was chosen was the fall of Margaret Thatcher rather than the election of 1992, but some observations on post-Thatcher Conservatism are included in the chapter dealing with Thatcher's rule and in the concluding chapter.

Whilst Parliamentary debates, government papers and political diaries and autobiographies have been consulted, the main sources for this book have been other accounts of the policies and politics of the era. This has been a period about which an enormous number of contemporary accounts and analyses have been provided. These have grown in volume, and the changes of the Thatcher era in particular have been the subject of a wide range of attempts at analysis, much of it very partisan.

Another feature of a book like this is that personal recall has obviously played a part, with its inevitable biases. For an author whose life has not been sufficiently important or interesting to write an autobiography, to write an account of events in his own lifetime which he has observed closely, and often passionately, and some of which have had a considerable impact upon his own life is the next best thing. I was a pre-war baby who grew up to enjoy many of the benefits of the social policy developments of the 1940s. Amongst those has been the sense of belonging to a caring society. I have been employed by the state almost all my working life, with experience in the employment service and in social security before moving into higher education. My wife has worked in the health service, my children and their partners all work in parts of the public sector with which this book is concerned. We are a family who are closely involved with the welfare state, happily more than anything else as employees of it. The contemporary Right regularly denigrates the efforts of the public servants who work to uphold the ideals of the welfare state. However we, and the overwhelming majority of our colleagues, remain committed to those ideals. That commitment has inevitably influenced the tone of this book, and particularly its concern to explain the factors which have limited, and recently set back, the achievements of social policy in Britain. Whilst it is hoped that this has been done with detachment, this project is influenced by a sense that the record could have been better. The book is dedicated to my grandchildren in the hope that the ideals of the welfare state will be advanced once again in their lifetimes.

Acknowledgements

I am grateful to Edward Elgar for commissioning this book, and to Julie Leppard for seeing it through the production process. Betty Hill and John Veit Wilson have taken a warm interest in the venture, and their comments on the manuscript have been invaluable in shaping the final product. Finally, I am very grateful for the assistance with the final preparation of the manuscript provided by Margaret Tulip and Julie Leppard.

1   Introduction

Introduction

This book looks at the political history of British social policy since 1945. It is in a sense a post-welfare state history, to put it rather contentiously, since for many people the 1945-51 governments are seen as the creators of the welfare state. This statement, which will be defended in the next chapter, indicates a central preoccupation of the book. This preoccupation arises from the fact that, while the period between 1945 and the present day has been very much one in which the welfare state was both consolidated and seemed to have its limits defined, the various political histories available (Morgan, 1990; Childs, 1986; Hennessy and Seldon, eds., 1987) have given social policy comparatively little attention.

Perhaps such authors take their cues from the fact that, whilst social policy expenditure has increasingly dominated public expenditure since 1945, the social policy ministries have remained comparatively low in the political pecking order. Until the creation of super ministries in the late 1960s, the social policy ministries were often not even directly represented in the British Cabinet and, even today, the social ministers rank low in the ministerial hierarchy.

There seems to be a paradox that whilst there has been a tendency to see the years in political terms as the period of the creation of the welfare state and the later part as a period of crisis for the welfare state, the main actors in the political arena have been seen as less significant than those of their colleagues concerned with economics, foreign affairs, defence and even law and order.

It will be suggested that this subordination of social policy, which continued until the 1970s, had rather different effects for the behaviour of the two major parties, effects which reduced the significance of their apparent ideological differences.

As far as the Labour party is concerned the political history of social policy since 1945 is one of a failure to achieve all that was promised and of inadequacy in the face of the policy problems with which it seemed to expect to deal. These failures can only be explained by relating social policy goals to economic and external affairs goals and aspirations. Hence, whilst the idea that social policy goals have to be curbed in an economically under-achieving nation with continuing aspirations to a 'world role' may seem to be a modern theme, belonging to the 1970s and 1980s, and particularly emphasised in the anti-welfare state rhetoric of Thatcherism, it will be suggested in this book that it is a theme which underlies the whole of the post-1945 period. Accounts of the 1945-51 Labour government (Morgan, 1984; Cairncross, 1985) have suggested that social policy got off to a good start then since so many of the fears of a repeat of the economic experience of the post-First World War period were not realised. Yet economic management at that time was not easy, and the American aid which got Britain through was bought at the price of longer-run political autonomy, in both external and internal affairs.

Very soon, for example, the political dispute over the need for social policy cuts to pay for rearmament in 1950-51 provides a clear illustration of the above theme. Subsequently, perhaps the major Labour intellectual/politician of the era, Anthony Crosland, set out the view that social policy is dependent upon economic growth in his book *The Future of Socialism* published in 1956, a view he underlined later in office in a social spending ministry when he warned local authorities in 1975 that 'the party is over'.

Contrastingly the Conservatives' record was never as anti-welfare as their rhetoric. One false image of this period is one that simply presents Labour as creating and the Conservatives as dismantling the welfare state. Whilst the forces which held back Labour creativity were economic and foreign policies, it is necessary to turn rather more to political theories to explain the inhibition of Conservative negativism. There are questions to be answered here about the electoral risks the Conservatives would have run had they done more to curb welfare expenditure. Some theories put this even more strongly as a risk of social unrest (Piven and Cloward, 1972). There are also some interesting issues about the extent to which bureaucratic and professional interests within the welfare state contributed to its advance and have been able to protect it. In this respect the subordination of social policy meant that the Conservatives were at times willing to leave the management of the welfare state to the 'permanent government' of the civil service, whilst they gave their attention to the 'high politics' which really interested them. Then, the Thatcher governments brought this to an end under a leader with a strong interest in the minutiae of domestic politics (Kavanagh, 1990, p.284).

The above propositions about the forces acting upon the major British political parties illustrate the underlying concerns of this book. Those concerns relate to a range of arguments in the political sociology of the welfare state. Those arguments have particularly dealt with the explanation of the origins of the welfare state, but have inevitably also been used to try to explain what sustains it, what limits it and, where relevant, what has or may undermine it.

Many of these arguments can only be effectively explored through comparative studies and by taking a long view of history. This is a book about one country over a comparatively short period of time, a time moreover after many of the relevant formative events had taken place. It cannot therefore claim to make a major contribution to the evaluation of these arguments. It does, however, need to be informed by them. Moreover, as the works of Ashford (1986) and of Heclo (1974) have shown, it is necessary to engage in a careful examination of specific events in social policy history to test the plausibility of some of these theories. It is also necessary to recognise that specific events may be need to be explained in terms of specific political processes embedded in a wider framework.

Macro-theory of the Welfare State

There have been extensive attempts in comparative work to identify broad determinants of welfare state growth (for recent discussions of this large literature see Esping-Andersen, 1990, ch.1; and Ashford, 1986). The problem with much of this theory is its low-level of specificity; hence it is of little use for this account. Such theory suggests that welfare states have emerged in societies with high levels both of industrialisation and of democratic participation. These two are related, and at a slightly lower level of generality it has been recognised that high levels of political mobilisation of manual workers tend to have occurred in those societies with advanced social policies. At this level of analysis there has been scope for historians and political scientists to engage in detailed exploration of the extent to which it is possible to argue that this labour mobilisation has been responsible for the social policy development (Esping-Andersen, 1990; Castles and McKinlay, 1979).

At this stage it should be pointed out that the question as to whether Britain should be regarded as a welfare state has so far been begged. In the 1950s British writers had little hesitation about this usage. Later, doubts crept in. One American comparative work describes Britain as a 'social security' state, contrasting it with the Swedish 'welfare state' (Furniss and Tilton, 1977). However, for the purposes of this discussion, all that needs to be accepted is that Britain belongs to that group of advanced industrial nations in which elaborate state-subsidised social policies have been built up. This group of states is widely defined as welfare states without the reservations implied in Furniss and Tilton's distinction.

The argument about the political mobilisation of labour is clearly relevant to this book. There is a body of, now rather old, literature which sees the British welfare state as a key achievement of the labour movement (for example, Marshall, 1965). This is an interpretation of the events between 1945 and 1951 to which the Labour Party leadership of that time undoubtedly subscribed. More recently this has been challenged in two ways. First, as comparative studies have shown that the British social policy achievement has, in the long run, compared unfavourably with the Scandinavian one, it has come to be argued that the supreme cases of labour movement achievement lie in those Northern countries and not in Britain. In this account attention will naturally be given to Labour's aspirations in social policy. There will be an examination of the ideological form those aspirations took, involving a desire to create comprehensive policies accessible to all and unregulated by means tests. Their difficulties in realising this 'universalist' ideal will be examined.

The second, perhaps more fundamental, challenge to theories about the influence of labour movements has come from analysts who have shown how strong other political forces can be. Examples have included work which draws attention to the role of Catholic social movements, in Austria for example (see Mishra, 1984), and work which analyses the importance of agrarian movements in alliance with the labour movement in Scandinavia (Baldwin, 1990). Neither of these critiques is relevant to Britain, but comparativists (Ashford, 1986; Baldwin, 1990) have shown that in the British case it is very important to bear in mind anti-industrial, paternalist and even collectivist tendencies in the Conservative Party.

However, there is another strain of theoretical and comparative work on the origins of the welfare state which has no difficulty with the idea that conservative politicians and capitalist interests have played a key role in the development of the welfare state. There is evidence from the end of the nineteenth century of conservative politicians and ideologues arguing that welfare institutions must be developed to 'tame' the new urban mob, to secure the support of the newly enfranchised electorate and to undermine the appeal of the emergent Marxist ideology. Bismarck, a German conservative and nationalist, is seen as the key example of a conservative progenitor of welfare, while one of the most characteristic European social policy instruments - social insurance - was developed as a device to give workers a 'stake' in the status quo.

This theoretical approach may be used to explain modern British Conservatism's support of the welfare state, but it is of course a generalised proposition which offers us no 'handle' with which to analyse specific events. However, this theory has been elaborated by some neo-Marxist writers (O'Connor, 1973; Gough, 1979; Offe, 1984) who have seen social welfare policy as the 'tribute' capital has had to pay to labour to stave off the crisis of capitalism predicted by Marx. But they have argued that problems for capitalism flow from this. One is that, over time, the price to be paid for social and industrial peace tends to rise. This follows logically from the Marxist argument that such measures postpone rather than abolish the realisation of the capitalist crisis (Wolfe, 1977). Here then, it is suggested, is a force which drives welfare expenditure ever upwards.

This part of the Marxist argument does little more than indicate a reason why all advanced capitalist states have developed welfare institutions and have found, once they have done so, that welfare expenditure tends to increase steadily. However, alternative explanations for this growth can be found in the rising political expectations of citizens. Theorists at the other end of the political spectrum from the Marxists have drawn attention to the extent to which democratic politics can involve an auction in which party competition to win elections drives up social expenditure, particularly when the costs can be hidden, delayed or spread (see Tullock, 1976; Brittan, 1977). In addition demographic changes may increase the numbers in the 'dependant' groups in the population, particularly elderly people. These are issues to be explored further in this book.

However, both Marxist and New Right theory go on to argue that welfare expenditure tends to be pushed up to a point at which a crisis arises. Welfare expenditure is unproductive, it is dependent upon the productive part of the economy. It is argued that the imposition of increasing welfare costs threatens the latter's efficiency and competitiveness with those economies which do not have to support welfare states. It has been argued that social policy places demands upon state investment which tend to crowd out investment in productive enterprise (Bacon and Eltis, 1976). It is also argued that the levels of taxation required to support social policies stifle enterprise (Joseph and Sumption, 1979).

It will be found that, in Britain, there was indeed a phase in welfare state history in the 1970s when theories of this kind were widely debated. There were also governmental responses which have been seen as involving recognition of this 'crisis'. The theories referred to above, and particularly the Marxist one, tend to be rather deterministic in nature.

There are grounds for distrusting them (Hill and Bramley, 1986) and for arguing that perhaps such 'crisis' as has occurred may have been rather more a crisis of confidence in collective action. It was a political rather than an economic crisis. What will be found in the account provided in this book is evidence that key actors believed there was a crisis which they had to do something about. In this sense there is no need to engage in an argument about whether the theorists were right or wrong. Politicians and administrators believed there was a crisis and acted upon their views of the right way to respond to it. The media disseminated propositions about the crisis and the public, or at least enough of the public to create support for the actions taken, accepted them.

Middle and Lower Range Theory

Classically the main form of theory in political science offering an approach to the explanation of specific events is pluralism. This is an elaboration of the more simplistic forms of democratic theory which expect political choice to be determined by the action of individual voters. Pluralists stress that our political behaviour takes place in groups - political parties, trade unions, pressure groups. Political outcomes are a result of competition between those groups. In the ideal pluralist world we all participate in the full range of relevant groups and a democratic outcome is realised since in the long run the balance of group forces is equivalent to the balance of individual interests (Dahl, 1961). In practice many pluralist theorists today recognise that the system may not be so balanced, that some interests are better able to enforce their wills than others (see, for example, Lindblom, 1977). Concepts of 'mobilisation of bias' and 'non-decision making' have been added to the armoury of pluralist concepts (Bachrach and Baratz, 1970).

What differentiates pluralist political science in methodological terms from its more holistic rivals is the belief that specific political decisions can be explained through the study of the participating actors. Pluralist theory, therefore, requires us to give attention to the activities of the political parties, their ideologies and the nature of their support. But it also suggests that we must have regard to their relationships with pressure groups. Much of the discussion in this book will look at the development of policy in these terms.

However, much pluralist theory tends to treat the state as if it is a passive recipient of outside pressures upon it (Nordlinger, 1981). There has been a reaction against this theoretical weakness in recent years with a body of work which has sought to 'bring the state back in' (Evans,

Rueschemeyer and Skocpol, eds., 1985). This is an important consideration for the study of social policy, since the establishment of the welfare state has involved the creation of a large bureaucratic and professional workforce which now has distinct *interests* of its own which it is likely to try to advance and defend both through participation in 'externalised' political debates and through political action within the state.

Interestingly both of the main currents in macro-theory discussed in the last section have sought to come to terms with this issue. The Marxists have developed the concept of the 'relative autonomy' of the state. For some theorists this principally involves a role for the state in the pursuit of the wider goals of capitalism in opposition to the efforts of specific 'fractions' to gain control, but for others this implies the pursuit of state interests separate from those of capitalism (see discussion in Dunleavy and O'Leary, 1987). But again, for the purposes of this book, it is perhaps the theory which has emanated from the New Right which is more interesting. This theory sees state bureaucrats as monopoly, or near monopoly, producers of services who are able to evade those market forces which are deemed to maximise efficiency and curb unnecessary organisational growth (Tullock, 1976). Such an emphasis clearly recognises that within the state there are some important interest groups. It may beg some questions about the direction in which interests may take their organisations and also disregard the extent that there are already some forms of competition within the state, but it draws our attention sharply to an important influence upon policy. It will be shown that New Right theory has played a part in the challenge, developed in the 1980s, to traditional ways of delivering state services.

But there is more to 'bringing the state back in' than simply recognising the importance of interests within the state. An earlier theory of the state - elitism - stressed the extent to which the state may be dominated by a small cohesive group with a distinct culture and value system of its own (Mosca, 1939; Mills, 1956). In examining the performance of the British welfare state, there is a need to recognise that the interventions involved in its creation were the product of an elite, dominant in Parliament and the civil service which had a specific set of beliefs about both the scope for and the limits to collective action, as well as about the appropriate forms intervention should take (for example, a strong commitment to centralism) (Ashford, 1986). Considerable attention has been given to the culture of this group in explaining the so-called consensus of 1945, suggesting that was enormously important in setting Britain on a course which was at one and the same time pro-welfare and anti-enterprise (Barnett, 1986; Wiener, 1981).

These ideas lead on to some interesting questions about the extent to which either efforts to modernise and open up state institutions in the 1960s and 1970s or the more total attack upon the public sector and its traditional ethos in the 1980s reflect, or have sought to produce, changes to this culture. In particular the institutional changes of the 1980s can be seen as trying to unleash incentives, either through competition or at least through the quantitative evaluation of performance, which would assist the process of replacing that culture by a more business-oriented one.

Towards Integrated Theory

It will be contended in the next chapter that when Labour came to power in 1945 the main battle over the development of the welfare state was more or less over. Many key interventions had occurred in the period between 1906 and 1939. During the Second World War itself, the Beveridge Report had been more or less accepted as providing the main direction for social security, and legislation for Family Allowances had already been accepted. Efforts were also already being made to create a health service.

Given its starting point, therefore, this is not a book which seeks to explain *why* the British welfare state came about, but rather one that deals with the form it took and the way that form evolved over the years after its creation. Therefore, prima facie, micro-theory, concerned with the explanation of specific events, is more likely to be useful here than macro-theory, dealing with broad tendencies in the evolution of the state. There will therefore be an emphasis compatible with the pluralist *methodology*, raising questions about the various actors participating in key decisions. But it is emphasised that it is pluralist methodology rather than pluralist theory which will be dominant. It is considered vital not to forget the extent to which wider factors - in the power structure, the nature of the economy and the evolution of society - set limits to the choices open to actors.

In the study of social policy it is important to acknowledge the differences between various policy issues. Attention has been drawn to the extent to which conflict particularly arises with policies which are redistributive (Lowi, 1972; Austin, 1983). While more policies are likely to be redistributive than they appear to be on superficial scrutiny, the key point is that there are some policies whose impact involves the production of identifiable gainers or losers, or providers and recipients, in the short run. In these cases structured politics involving major class and other interest groups will be manifest, and ideological standpoints are likely to be taken, particularly by political parties.

Yet even when looking at these major policy issues, there is a need to be sensitive to subtle shifts in the agenda. First, as various opinion studies have shown (see Taylor-Gooby, 1985), there is an important difference between those policies for which there is widespread support and therefore presumably tolerance of the redistribution of costs (such as pensions and the health service) and those where there is considerable evidence of suspicion and hostility (such as benefits for unemployed people or single parents). Second, in the day-to-day processes of policy-making, the agenda may shift from the macro to the micro, as happened for example to the debate over the health service as attention moved from whether a service should be provided to how it should be provided. In the long run, as this example suggests, the micro-politics of the roles to be played by various professionals and by various tiers of government may be just as important as the macro-politics of redistribution.

Lowi, in his typology referred to above, also discusses what he calls 'constituent policy' concerned with the formulation and re-formulation of the machinery of government. Such policy figures prominently both in the setting up of the institutions of the modern welfare state and in their subsequent modification. There have been major preoccupations, for example, about whether the structure of the health service is right and about the role of local government in policy delivery. There has been a growing recognition that an important influence upon 'who gets what' in social policy depends upon how the implementation structure is set up. This in turn has an impact upon the way various bureaucratic and professional groups are able to determine policy outputs. It also influences access from citizens and their advocates. In the course of the book a shift of attention will be evident from directly 'redistributive' to 'constituent' policies, not forgetting that the latter will nevertheless have redistributive effects. This is partly a response to public expenditure constraints, requiring resources to be used more effectively. It is also partly a consequence of a developing sophistication on these issues which seems to have been rather absent from the early debates about social policy. It is also finally an ideological response, manifested as a growing unwillingness to leave public bureaucracy to get on with the job of delivering benefits and services (for reasons discussed above).

Hence, this book will endeavour to analyse many, but of course by no means all, of the key events in the political history of British social policy since 1945, using a variety of conceptual and theoretical tools derived from political science and political sociology and informed by the controversy over the origins of welfare states which has engaged theorists, particularly comparativists, over the recent past. It will give particular attention to three themes which will be reviewed carefully in the concluding chapter. These are:

(1) The nature of social expenditure trends over the period, and the factors which may explain them. Included within this is the issue concerning the extent to which political party control over the government influences expenditure trends (see Rose, 1984).

(2) The relevance of party ideology for policy outcomes, here a division of views about universalism in social policy will be examined to see to what extent it had an impact upon how policies were designed by the two main political parties when in government.

(3) The importance of political processes outside the party political conflict, concerning the influence of bureaucrats and professionals and the relationship between central and local government. Two sub-themes here are the extent to which the dominance of permanent officials contributed to a consensus in many policy areas, and the extent to which the 'constituent policies' of institutional change were designed to disturb that consensus.

2   Social Policy before 1945

Introduction

In planning this book it was difficult to decide what year the historical account should start. During the Second World War several events occurred which were important for subsequent social policy history. So it could perhaps have started in 1939. In the middle of the war the publication of the Beveridge Report in 1942 was a crucial milestone for social policy. There was a strong temptation to start then. In the end it was decided that it was better to start a political history from the General Election of 1945, the end of the peculiar politics of coalition government and the beginning of the two-party conflict which has characterised post war-politics. In an historical narrative any starting point poses difficulties because of the importance for the future of the past. These difficulties make necessary a chapter like this one in which crucial earlier events are sketched in and an effort made to ensure that readers understand the context of the events to be described in the following chapters.

One special problem about taking 1945 as the starting date for an account of government activities in respect of domestic policies is that it marks the end of such an exceptional period for the government and nation. Throughout this book issues about social policy expenditure levels will be examined in relation to overall levels of government expenditure, the level of national prosperity (as measured by the Gross Domestic Product - GDP - an indicator of the level of production of goods and services) and the level of taxation. It will be recognised from the attention given to the 'welfare state crisis' theory in the previous chapter that it is important to measure the development of social policy in these terms. Yet at the starting point of 1945, these figures were all peculiarly distorted by the impact of the war on government and the economy. In 1945 public expenditure (including 'transfer' payments of benefits and subsidies to individuals and companies) was about 55 per cent of GDP (Feinstein, 1972, Tables 14 and 19), with social policy expenditure constituting about 5 per cent of total expenditure (Butler and Sloman, 1980, p.356). The standard rate of income tax was 50 per cent

11

(ibid. p.348). It may be argued therefore that the transition from war to peace could involve a substantial replacement of military expenditure by social expenditure; indeed it will be suggested that this shift reduced the extent to which social policy was seen, in the early years after the war, as a threat to public expenditure. However for many people at the time a more appropriate reference point was the pre-war level of expenditure. In 1938 public expenditure was about 21 per cent of GDP (Feinstein, 1972) with social policy expenditure constituting about 15 per cent of the total (Butler and Sloman, 1980, p.356). The standard rate of income tax was 25 per cent (ibid. p.348). These obviously offer very different yardsticks for the measurement of post-war expenditure. Perhaps the ideal comparators are somewhere between the two. In 1945 people seeking the restoration of a peacetime society, but there was a very widespread view that the 1930s, with its high unemployment, considerable social unrest and looming 'war clouds', was not an era to look back to with nostalgia or to copy.

In this chapter an account will first be provided of the main characteristics of those social policies already in place by the 1945 election. Then three crucial developments which occurred during the war will be considered: the Beveridge Report, the 'Butler' Education Act of 1944 and the early moves towards the establishment of a national health service. This will be followed by an examination of what may be described as the 'mood of 1945' - the political and social atmosphere of the time. Finally, some comments will be made about the political and institutional context in which the policy decisions of the post-war period were made.

Social Policy in 1945

A series of social policy innovations made in the early years of the century had been consolidated in the inter-war period. Most low-income male earners were contributors to a social insurance scheme which provided limited flat-rate pensions, sickness benefits and unemployment benefits, together with primary medical care for themselves. Prolonged unemployment during the inter-war period had considerably undermined the insurance benefit scheme for the unemployed, but in 1934 the government had set up the Unemployment Assistance Board (UAB) to administer a national means-tested benefit scheme for those out of work so that they did not need to apply to the Poor Law. In 1940 and 1941 the government had extended the role of the UAB to cover the needs of other groups, such as the elderly poor, and renamed it the Assistance Board. Hence, most of the work of the Poor Law had already been taken away.

The Poor Law had been brought under the control of local authority Public Assistance Committees in 1929; released from most cash assistance duties, these bodies had extended their hospital and residential care provisions.

The overall situation with regard to health care remained confused and complicated. Insurance contributors, normally males in full-time manual work, benefited from a system of primary care, which might include a range of ancillary services if they were insured by flourishing Assurance Societies. Yet their families would still have to pay for medical services or seek help from charitable hospitals or the Poor Law. Hospital services came under the control of an unplanned mixture of voluntary and local authority hospitals (many of the latter just emerging from the stigma of the Poor Law) in the pre-war period. During the war the government established some measure of control over the whole hospital system, under the Emergency Medical Service, in order to be able to deal efficiently with war casualties.

Personal social services, as we identify them today, were still very rudimentary in nature. In this area of social policy the Poor Law remained the key source of help, offering institutional care for elderly and handicapped people and for abandoned children. Progressive local health authorities had developed some domiciliary care facilities to help with confinements (most children were born at home in those days). These authorities also provided domiciliary midwives, home nurses and health visitors. Education authorities had also started to provide a range of 'welfare' services. To assist the mobilisation of females for war work, local authorities had been subsidised to provide day nurseries. Overall, developments were very patchy and ad hoc, and there was some expectation that many of these services which had been provided to deal with 'emergencies' like war work, the evacuation of children and the disruption of homes by the war would decline with the coming of peace.

In the period before the First World War housing was predominantly provided by private owners for rent. In the inter-war period the system had begun to evolve towards its modern form. A number of Acts of Parliament had subsidised local authorities to provide housing. At the same time an extensive private building programme of houses for sale had extended owner-occupation. Both of these developments had then been retarded by the war, when no new houses were built and many old ones were damaged by bombs. The Coalition Government had promised an extensive building programme once the war was ended. In 1945 12 per cent of households were in local authority tenancies, 26 per cent were owner-occupiers and 54 per cent were tenants of private landlords. 8 per cent were in 'other' tenancies, mainly tied housing.

The education system offered free primary education for all, but secondary opportunities were limited, with scholarships available for only a minority of able lower middle-class and working-class children. The further and higher education sectors were very small, with only 69,000 British people (compared with about ten times as many by the end of the 1980s) in full-time higher education in 1938-9 (see Halsey ed., 1988, p.270). The war had, of course, considerably disrupted education.

Inevitably employment policy was a major preoccupation of the war-time planners for peace. The inter-war period had seen nearly continuous high levels of unemployment. The lowest annual average unemployment rate was 7.4 per cent in 1927. The highest rate was 17 per cent in 1932. The rate was well over 10 per cent continuously from 1930 to 1936 (Feinstein, 1972, Table 58). Unemployment only really fell sharply in the period when Britain was arming for war. The Labour Exchange system, set up in 1909, proved useful for the administration of benefits for the unemployed but could seldom play any more positive role. One small change to its role as a result of war-time legislation was the development of a system of help for disabled people, involving a quota system and special counselling and training services. This was a specific response to the labour needs of the war-time period and the expectation of a large number of war-disabled people.

By the end of the 1930s there had emerged some attempts to create jobs and to use planning devices to stimulate employment in the most disadvantaged regions, but this development was rudimentary. The war more or less abolished unemployment (indeed when statements are made today about the size of the so- called 'unemployable' population it is instructive to note how few seemed to fall into that category in war-time). But the problem of unemployment was expected to re-emerge after the war. Just as generals are often alleged to be fighting the previous war, so the planners for peace expected the economic disruption which had followed the First World War occur again. At the end of the 1930s new approaches to the management of the economy, stimulated by the theories of Maynard Keynes, had began to get on the political agenda, but by 1945 they had not been fully accepted. On the whole the main alternative to the return to the economic status quo was seen as the continuation of the sort of 'directive' economic planning which had been adopted during the war.

The Beveridge Report

The Beveridge Report was a product of one of a number of efforts to plan for the forthcoming peace. It was accepted within the Coalition Government that there would be a need to rationalise and improve income maintenance policy after the war. But the Beveridge Report seems to have been something of a surprise, even an unwelcome surprise to the Prime Minister, Winston Churchill, for whom any government preoccupation with policies for the post-war period got in the way of single-minded concentration on the war effort. Judging by Harris' account (1977) William Beveridge, who had participated in social policy development before the First World War and had held high office during that war but had then been in senior academic posts between the wars, was given this forward planning task to keep him out of more immediate planning activities. He then succeeded in securing a high profile for his activities, promising a 'blue-print for the future'. Through talks, articles and lobbying he had created an atmosphere of high anticipation before the report was published. He then had the good fortune that it was published at a time of optimism for the future, after the military success in the battle of El Alamein (Addison, 1975).

The report itself was a combination of quite detailed proposals for a comprehensive social insurance system and some influential rhetoric on future social policy needs.

The latter described the road to social reconstruction after the war as involving 'slaying the five giants' of 'Want, Disease, Ignorance, Squalor and Idleness'. More specifically it laid down three conditions necessary for the development of a satisfactory system of income maintenance: the introduction of a system of family allowances, the setting up of a comprehensive health and rehabilitation service and the maintenance of full employment. In some respect these accompanying conditions made more political impact than the social insurance proposals themselves. As will be seen below, work was already starting on the development of proposals for a health service, Beveridge's remarks further stimulated this. The family allowances proposal was in fact adopted by the Coalition Government, which enacted legislation early in 1945 to provide 5 shillings (25 pence) a week for the second and subsequent children in all families (to put figures like this in perspective, it should be borne in mind that the average male manual worker's wage at this time was about £6). This was not implemented until after Labour came to power. As already mentioned the prevention of unemployment in the post-war period was, a key preoccupation as politicians anticipated peace. In fact, Beveridge's concept of 'full employment' was, by post-war standards, a modest one - eight and a half per cent.

The social insurance proposals involved the payment of flat-rate benefits to pensioners, widows, the sick and the unemployed. Flat rate in this sense meant fixed sums for individuals with additions for dependants, with no graduation in relation to past earnings. These were to be funded by flat-rate contributions from the insured, their employers and the state. This was very much the universalisation of the pre-existing insurance scheme; hence, as Baldwin (1990) has argued, its principal beneficiaries were the previously excluded middle-class. There was a crucial issue here about the rate at which the scheme should be phased in. Beveridge recommended that new contributors should have to wait 20 years to earn a full pension, a recommendation which the Labour Government rejected. Another critical issue for any judgement about the extent to which the Beveridge recommendations were 'revolutionary' concerns the rates of benefit proposed. Veit Wilson (1992) has shown that Beveridge was very cautious on this issue, making use of Rowntree's earlier studies of poverty (1901, 1918, 1937, 1941) but interpreting them in a way which implied benefits below a minimum that Rowntree would have regarded as reasonable, and failing to take effective account of the implications of housing costs. In other words, Beveridge's social insurance proposals were really quite conservative. They involved continuity with the past, a high proportion of funding from contributions rather than directly from taxation and very modest benefit levels.

Alongside the main insurance benefits, Beveridge proposed a more generous scheme for the compensation of victims of industrial injuries and accidents, substantially supplanting the earlier litigation-based system. He also proposed an assistance scheme for those not adequately covered by social insurance. He (incorrectly as will be seen) predicted that this would be of importance only during a transitional period. This, of course, was merely a development of the existing task of the Assistance Board to facilitate the final abolition of the Poor Law. Finally, he proposed that the whole scheme should be the responsibility of a unified Ministry of Social Security.

Given the symbolic importance of the Beveridge Report it is necessary to look at the politics of its reception. The Labour Party, in the main, received it enthusiastically. The only significant exception to this was continuing trade union suspicion about family allowances, which were seen as an attack on wages. This was voiced within the Coalition by the union leader, Ernest Bevin. The rank and file of the Labour Party pressed strongly for the Report's acceptance, and various independent and

Commonwealth Party by-election candidates who were carrying the political 'flag' of the Left (in the face of an electoral pact which prevented Labour contestants in Tory held seats in by-elections) made it central to their platforms (see Addison, 1975, pp.225-6).

Churchill, as was suggested above, regarded all this as a distraction from the war effort. Some business interests inside and outside the Conservative party actively opposed the Report, and the Chancellor of the Exchequer, Kingsley Wood, whose department had already been influential in limiting Beveridge's proposals, warned of their cost. Some of Churchill's colleagues - notably Lord Beaverbrook and Brendan Bracken - were alarmed at Beveridge's immediate propaganda successes, including the wide publication and extensive dissemination of his ideas within the armed forces.

Clearly, inasmuch as there was a division between the political parties, the Report created dissension within the Coalition (see Addison, 1975, pp.220-25). However, it also created dissension within the Conservative party since a significant group of younger Members, the Tory Reform Committee, supported its adoption. The Conservative party came to accept the broad thrust of the Report. It has already been noted that the Coalition enacted the family allowances proposal before it broke up. This is particularly interesting since this was an element that was to be entirely tax-funded and has come to be seen by many on the Right as an unnecessarily universalist, and costly, element in the income maintenance package. Overall, the Coalition Government published a White Paper broadly accepting the Beveridge proposals, while in its manifesto for the 1945 election the Conservative party pledged to implement them.

The 'Butler' Education Act of 1944

While there is less to be said about the 1944 Education Act than there is about the Beveridge Report, it is also an interesting manifestation of the peculiar politics of the war-time Coalition Government. R. A. (Rab) Butler was one of the younger Conservative politicians in the Coalition. He had been closely associated with 'appeasement' in the pre-war period so, as an ambitious politician, he had something to live down. When Churchill appointed him to the Board of Education (to become a Ministry under the 1944 Act) he clearly expected him, as a good administrator, to devote himself to the detailed problems of running the disrupted education service (Howard, 1987). Butler himself quoted Churchill's briefing to him on becoming President of the Board of Education as follows:

'I think you can leave your mark there. You will be independent. Besides', he continued with rising fervour, 'you will be in the war. You will move poor children from here to here', and he lifted up and evacuated imaginary children from one side of his blotting pad to the other; 'this will be very difficult' (Butler in Fowler et al., eds., 1973, p.4).

However, Butler saw the need to reconstruct the education system to make it a more unified and progressive force in peacetime. At first Churchill's reaction was rather like his response to Beveridge. He had little interest in education policy and he certainly did not want his government to do anything which would excite the various religious lobbies with an interest in education. Butler quotes a minute from Churchill, sent in September 1941, which was initially interpreted as a prime ministerial veto:

> It would be the greatest mistake to raise the 1902 controversy during the war, and I certainly cannot contemplate a new education bill.... No one can possibly tell what the financial and economic state of the country will be when the war is over. Your main task at present is to get the schools working as well as possible under all the difficulties of air attack, evacuation, etc (ibid. p.5).

Churchill gave in, some time later, after extensive preparatory work by Butler. Addison suggests (1975, p.238) that Butler succeeded partly because education reform could be seen as a Conservative contribution to reconstruction alongside the Beveridge Report, and partly because the costs of reform were well in the future and were unclear in quantity (unlike those entailed in the enactment of the Beveridge Report's proposals)(see Butler in Fowler et al., eds., 1973, p.19).

The 1944 Act raised the minimum school-leaving age to 15 (but note that this was not implemented until 1947), and it made state education in secondary schools free. It made provision for higher levels of state support for some categories of religious controlled schools by means of a compromise measure which enabled such schools to choose either an almost entirely local authority funded status ('controlled') or a less controlled but less well funded status ('voluntary aided'). It guaranteed the inclusion of religious education and a communal act of worship in the syllabus.

Under the Act a division between primary and secondary education was expected. The standard view, at the time, was of primary education from 5 to 11 and of secondary education from 11 to 18 (with the option of leaving after 15). This was to lead to the general adoption of a selection process based upon tests at 11 plus, to allocate children either to 'grammar' schools for the 'academic' or secondary modern schools for the rest (there were also tri-partite versions of this model, with 'technical' schools in the 'middle'). This was not mandatory under the Act, but it was received opinion at that time that children had distinctly different genetically determined attributes for which different forms of education provision were appropriate. Although challenged by some elements in the teaching profession and in the Labour Party, this 'orthodoxy' was ccepted by the Labour implementers of the Butler Act. Only later were rnative ideas adopted. The Butler Act provided a sufficiently flexible ure for this further educational innovation.

a National Health Service

ealth there was no Beveridge type blueprint which had gination of politicians before 1945 and no Coalition slation. Nevertheless the incoming Labour Government Coalition commitment to health service reform as well amount of preliminary work towards that reform, Paper published early in 1944 (Ministry of Health,).

the Minister of Health (and a Conservative MP), ting up of a health service in which free patient care ble from family practitioners, under contract to bodies e existing National Health Insurance Committees at the me evolution towards a salaried service. He proposed a m under local authority control, but with voluntary hospitals ir independence by working under contract. He worked ries of complex negotiations, most of which had not reached tion by the 1945 election (see Pater, 1981).

s proposals attracted the hostility of the doctors, who were to a salaried service, but seemed to satisfy the voluntary hospitals local authorities. There were, however, considerable difficulties be resolved about the administrative arrangements, given the small many local authorities. This was only the beginning of a battle became much more fierce once Aneurin Bevan introduced Labour's ation (discussed in the next chapter). Clearly the great achievement an was to negotiate his way through this mounting opposition. But mportant not to forget that the basic principle of a free and hensive health service, which had been sought by progressive ts within the medical profession and the Labour Party since the 920s, was conceded by a Conservative member of the Coalition ment.

The Mood of 1945

The three specific examples of the Beveridge Report, the Butler Act and
the Willink White Paper have been discussed both because they were very
important for the social policy developments to come and because they
provide significant evidence of the political drift of the Coalitio
Government at the end of the war. Here is the evidence for what
been described as the consensus of 1945. Addison's book, *The R*
1945, which has been one of the key sources for this chapter, de
what he calls the process by which Attlee's consensus replaced B
consensus. But some writers have gone further (Wiener, 19
1986), to suggest that there was not much discontinuity e
age of Baldwin and the age of Attlee. British Conserv
and (as will be shown) continued to contain after t
paternalistic commitment to 'one nation'. Key fi
Conservatism like Butler and Macmillan played a key
that tradition, judging Baldwin as having failed the tr
would have seen himself as heir. A fourth issue wh
very strongly, and was discussed in an earlier sectior
commitment to preventing unemployment in the post-w
  Of course, confronted with some of the economic di
faced after 1945, the Conservatives might have backed
reform. Equally Willink or his successor might not ha
doctors as skilfully as Bevan (but he might, of course, h
less!). One can speculate endlessly about the 'might ha
history. We can only read the Conservative manifesto f
election and try to deduce from that what they would have
indicates a wholehearted commitment to Beveridge, a natio
service and full employment, as these quotes make clear:

> One of our most important tasks will be to pass into law and bring ir
> as soon as we can a nation-wide and compulsory scheme of National I
> based on the plan announced by the Government of all Parties in 19

> The health services of the country will be made available to all
> Everyone will contribute to the cost, and no one will be denied the
> the treatment or the appliances he requires because he cannot affo

> The Government accepts as one of its primary aims and resp
> maintenance of a high and stable level of employment.

Labour won decisively, turning its back at last on its miserable electoral history in the inter-war period. Such opinion poll data as is available from that period shows that there was a strong commitment to social reform and presumably a belief that Labour was the party to carry it through (see Addison, 1975).

A less enthusiastic approach analysis of the mood of 1945 than Addison's is provided by Barnett (1986). He has written critically of the way in which the British people had become gripped by the 'new Jerusalem' perspective. He argues that

> If Britain after the war was to earn the immense resources required to maintain her cherished traditional place as a great power and at the same time pay for New Jerusalem at home, she had to achieve nothing short of an economic miracle (Barnett, 1986, p.237).

He believes that, on the contrary, there was 'a massive inertial resistance' to economic and industrial change which made such a miracle impossible. In his analysis the very nature of that resistance was part of the same ideology and culture which engendered the belief in state intervention to achieve 'New Jerusalem' in social policy.

The same theme is taken up in a rather different way by an American historian. Wiener (1981), in his analysis of the way in which the British bourgeoisie adopted aristocratic and rural values, shows in the 1940s both socialists and traditionalists embraced a belief in the capacity of social reform to usher in a more harmonious but also a more relaxed, backward-looking social order.

There are two points about this argument which are important for a political analysis of the emergence of the British version of the welfare state. One is that these writers show how much this commitment to a harmonious consensus came from an upper middle-class elite, with intellectuals and church leaders prominent in their ranks. Beveridge - an Oxford educated product of an Indian civil service family - was a very typical example. Another American, Ashford (1986), has drawn attention to the strong 'moral tone' of the British movement for social reform and has argued that 'the conceptual foundation of the British welfare state remained individual radicalism, not a form of social radicalism' (Ashford, p.305). Thus, he reminds us that the British reforms were not a product of fierce class conflict. They were not simply concessions seized from an unwilling ruling class.

The other point which this line of argument highlights is the lack of cultural or institutional change accompanying the process of reform. This is a theme which will be taken further later. It is important to examine the cultural and institutional framework which Labour inherited in 1945.

The 1945 Inheritance: Cultural and Institutional Issues

The first point to make in this section is banal, but nonetheless should not be forgotten. In 1945 Britain won a war, after six years of extensive sacrifices. Whilst it could not have won that war without the participation of others, notably the United States and the Soviet Union, for a significant period it did stand almost alone without help from these larger nations. On winning a war a nation is not in an appropriate frame of mind for an examination of its problems and weaknesses. Victory induced a mood of euphoria. Existing British values and institutions were believed to have triumphed. It may be said with the benefit of hindsight that the war period, and perhaps even more the period immediately before it, demonstrated many weaknesses in the British state. It may also be said that the war intensified some of those weaknesses. However, these were not conclusions which were being drawn in 1945.

The election of 1945 is notable, in that, despite war euphoria and despite the fact that the Conservative leader Winston Churchill was feted as a war hero, Labour won. This may seem to contradict what has been asserted above. But what was significant was that Labour, as a loyal member in the Coalition, had participated in the 'winning team'. Various commentators have referred to the way Churchill 'tastelessly' reverted to traditional electoral rhetoric in warning Britain against a socialist 'Gestapo'. Addison reports that Mass Observation commented: 'It would be difficult to exaggerate the disappointment and genuine distress aroused by this speech' (Addison, 1975 p.265). The Labour leaders were no longer seen as outsiders in British politics, they had proved by their participation in the Coalition, and by the statesmanlike way they conducted themselves on its breakup, that they had joined the 'establishment'. When, later, members of the Labour Government, and particularly Aneurin Bevan, behaved in ways which suggested they did not altogether see themselves in that way Attlee, the Prime Minister, was quick to condemn them.

What follows from all this is that the Labour Government, elected in 1945, was experienced in using the traditional machinery of Parliament and in working with the civil service. In the First World War the tasks of government had suddenly been vastly enlarged. This placed considerable strain on the institutions of government. New departments were set up. It was recognised that the Prime Minister and Cabinet needed direct civil service staffs and that there had to be a mechanism to integrate the whole system (Chapman and Greenaway, 1980, ch.2). The Treasury assumed that role.

During the Second World War there inevitably had to be institutional changes, and large numbers of temporary civil servants were imported into Whitehall. Yet the system was more prepared for this shock. It did not lead to any significant questioning of the machinery of government. After the war many of the 'temporaries' left quite quickly, and the system reverted to traditional ways of working (see Hennessy, 1989). The class composition of the permanent civil service was little affected by the upheaval, the public school and Oxbridge elite reasserted itself to remain unchallenged until Labour's later term of office in 1964-70. In fact even that challenge was largely resisted.

In other words the introduction of the new social policies was managed by a Labour Government, working harmoniously with a traditional civil service, with no interest in challenging existing ways of managing policies. A particular manifestation of this, to which Ashford has drawn attention, was the extent to which central government was distrustful of local government. Earlier governments dominated by landed aristocrats had resisted the replacement or the modernisation of the traditional local taxation system - rates levied upon the basis of the values of properties occupied. Accordingly as central government had demanded more of local government, it had found that it needed to increase steadily grant support from the centre. At the same time some local governments had come under radical Labour control, making increased demands upon the centre and further highlighting problems of territorial justice (Branson, 1979; Gilbert, 1970). The result was a central suspicion of local government, and therefore a predisposition to centralise. Manifestations of this in the 1945-51 period were the elimination of local government controlled utilities, but the case of particular importance for social policy concerned the organisation of the health service (see next chapter). Later in the book it will be shown how some problems about central-local government relations which were ignored in the 1940s reached crisis point for the politics of social policy in the 1980s.

Finally, one last feature of the 1945 cultural consensus very important for social policy decision-making was the incorporation of the professions into the administrative and managerial elite. There was no suggestion at this time that professional dominance might be a problem for emergent social policy. Accordingly, it will be found in the next chapter that the politics of a generally deferential relationship between government and medicine was of enormous importance in the development of the health service. Later chapters will also show that, for a remarkably long period, education decision-making proceeded as a professionalised process largely out of sight of the public. Later, the picture changed dramatically.

It is only easy with the benefit of hindsight to identify what was not changing in the 1940s, and the questions - particularly about institutional arrangements - which were not being asked. The society of the 1940s, as Morgan has shown most effectively, was a strange mixture of change and stability:

> It was, then, a comparatively conservative nation in which rapid legislative change and innovations in welfare were superimposed on a class and institutional structure which closely resembled pre-war years. Yet it was also, so it seemed, a generally content society, despite the austerity, deeply patriotic, certain of British greatness, and observing Empire Day in state schools every May with the same intensity as under the Raj (Morgan, 1990, p.108).

3   The Labour Governments 1945-51

Introduction

The Labour Party won power decisively in the General Election of July 1945. It took 393 Parliamentary seats to the Conservatives' 213. Other parties secured 34 seats. Labour won 47.8 per cent of the vote, the Conservatives 39.8 per cent (Butler and Sloman, 1980, p.208). This represented a massive swing to Labour since the last general election which, because of the war, had been ten years before. In 1935 Labour won only 37.9 per cent of the vote and 154 seats.

In the subsequent election of 1950 Labour narrowly held on to power, winning 315 seats to the Conservatives' 298. Other parties won 12 seats. Ill-health and internal dissension in the Labour Party made it difficult for it to defend this slender majority and the government eventually 'went to the country' again in October 1951 when it was defeated.

As indicated in the introductory chapter, no attempt will be made here to describe all the social policies of this or any subsequent government, in great detail. This introductory section provides an overview and a concluding section sums up the picture as a whole. In between, attention will be given to developments in the main areas of social policy, considering the main policy innovations and other political events which are regarded as particularly central to the political history of social policy in this period.

On coming to power, the government was worried that the state of national external indebtedness after the war would make it very difficult to fulfil its social policy pledges. Its difficulties were enhanced by the American decision to withdraw the Lease-Lend arrangement which had done so much to support the British war effort, immediately after the end of the war in the Far East. The government went through an anxious period while Treasury representatives negotiated a further loan from the United States, with the latter disinclined to offer the new government any special favours. Eventually they secured a loan which gave Britain the breathing space needed and which, with the benefit of hindsight, proved very favourable in terms of both the rate of interest and the repayment period (see discussion in Morgan, 1984, pp.143-51 and in Cairncross, 1985, Chapter 5).

An interesting feature of the politics of social policy in the 1945-51 period is that, despite the problem of external debt, the government had comparatively little difficulty achieving a budgeting surplus. Tax rates were very high and, for the first few years after the war defence, expenditure was rapidly reduced. Cairncross describes the situation as follows:

> As demobilisation proceeded, defence expenditure fell from £4.4 billion to £0.85 billion ... between 1945-6 and 1947-8 and changed little thereafter until rearmament in 1951-2. Expenditure on other supply services trebled over those first two years, rising from £0.6 billion to £1.8 billion and absorbing roughly one-third of the purchasing power released by the fall in defence expenditure. Tax revenue increased in spite of the reductions made in tax. Thus the swing in the budget balance was not far short of the falling-off in defence expenditure (Cairncross, 1985, p.420).

In other words there was a 'peace dividend' available to pay for social policy expansion. At the same time the government was not inclined to grant dramatic tax reductions. In fact high tax rates (with income tax having begun for the first time to bite into ordinary working class incomes during the war) helped, along with rationing, to rein in domestic demand through a period in which many shortages continued. Only one change was made in the standard rate of income tax: it was reduced from 50 per cent to 45 per cent in April 1946.

In later chapters of this book data will be quoted illustrating changes in the level of social expenditure under each government, and efforts will be made to compare governments. The data available for the 1940s are difficult to use in this way. Little material was published, and there was little concern to analyse trends in real terms or to enable comparisons to be made between departments. Feinstein's (1972) estimates of public expenditure as a proportion of GDP provide a broad overview of public expenditure trends during this period. They show that, once the nation had moved away from a war footing, public sector expenditure levels which were low compared with those of the 1970s and 1980s when levels between 40 and 50 per cent were recorded in most years. Figures derived from Feinstein's work are set out in Table 3.1.

Table 3.1   Estimates of Public Expenditure 1945-51 as a Percentage of
              GDP

	Public expenditure on goods and services	Transfer payments (gross)
1945	46.5	8.9
1946	25.7	13.1
1947	18.6	12.8
1948	17.3	12.5
1949	19.7	11.7
1950	18.9	10.9
1951	19.9	10.2

Source: Feinstein, Tables 2 and 14

In Table 3.1 transfer payments, that is payments of benefits or subsidies
(within which social security payments were a large element), have been
included 'gross', that is without taking into account income (as is
government practice in publishing public expenditure figures). They
nevertheless show a trend which was relatively unproblematic from the
point of view of Treasury concern about expenditure growth. At this time
a separate National Insurance account was maintained - within which
contributions from employees, employers and the government were
registered. This steadily increased its surplus after the passing of the
National Insurance Act (HMSO, 1951, Table 24 pp.36-7). The growth in
pensioner claimants, which was soon to worry the managers of the
scheme, had not really begun (see Phillips Report, Cmnd 6404, 1954).
It is also important to note that unemployment had remained at very low
levels.

The data on public expenditure from this period are difficult to dissect
in comparison with the data to be discussed in later chapters. Education
expenditure was kept under strict control. In this period issues about the

lack of resources for capital expenditure, for the building of new schools, assumed more significance than general problems of expenditure control. The section on housing will also show that shortages of materials played a bigger part in inhibiting expenditure growth than did Treasury controls. Later in this chapter some concerns about the growth of health expenditure will be examined. It was with the introduction of re-armament that there was the emergence of the continuing battle between the restrictive Treasury and the demanding social policy spending departments, with health in this case in the front-line, which will preoccupy much of the rest of this book. The last section before the overview will therefore look at the conflicts which occurred in 1950-51 over cuts in social expenditure in order to finance the costs of rearma-ment. Before that, various sections will examine the key social policy developments under the 1945-51 government.

Income Maintenance Policy: The Reform of Social Insurance

The government was pledged to introduce a social insurance scheme, based upon the proposals of the Beveridge Report. It introduced the National Insurance Bill at the end of 1945, the second reading debate in the House of Commons occurring on 6 February 1946. There is considerable evidence of what a low-key event this was in political terms. The minister responsible, James Griffiths, was not even a member of the Cabinet. In replying to Griffiths' introductory speech his 'shadow' on the Conservative side, Rab Butler, started:

> Friends on this side of the House have contributed our share to the making of this plan, and we wish to see it through... but... it is the duty of the Opposition to criticise (Hansard Vol. 418, Session 1945-46, p.1759).

Undoubtedly he had the 1944 White Paper in mind which, though less generous than Griffiths' proposals, was very much along the same lines. Some criticism of some of the more complex qualification rules came from the Left of the Labour Party, which secured concessions which slightly extended the benefits available to the unemployed. Overall, the passage of the Bill was comparatively untroubled.

Of course, much of the debate about the cost of this measure had gone on intermittently since the early days of the work of the Beveridge committee. Beveridge had taken Treasury views into account in determining the rates of benefit and contribution conditions which made it predominantly a 'pay as you go' scheme with only one-sixth of the cost carried by the state (except in the case of unemployment benefit where the notional state contribution was to be one-third). The 1944 White Paper took a similar line. Griffiths was a little more generous than either Beveridge or the White Paper on benefit rates, but there had been some increase in the cost of living by then. Moreover, the price for this was that Griffiths demanded higher contributions to maintain the ratio between the state's contribution and those from employees and employers.

There were two other important differences between the Beveridge design and the Act. Beveridge had envisaged an inexhaustible unemployment benefit scheme, with provisions for compulsory training to apply to the long-term unemployed. The Act provided for unemployment benefit to last only six months, with an extension to one year for those with comparatively good contribution records. On pensions Beveridge proposed that new entrants, who had not been in the previous social insurance scheme, should take 20 years to accumulate a full benefit entitlement. It was perhaps naive of Beveridge to expect that politicians would accept this delay; as Ellis puts it, 'Neither the Coalition nor post-war Government... regarded it as reasonable to keep benefit levels depressed for so long a period' (Ellis, 1989, p.3). The Act shortened it to ten years. Baldwin refers to this as evidence of the capacity of the well-off 'to alter Beveridge's proposals to their own specifications' (Baldwin, 1990, p.133). He cites no evidence of lobbying to this end. What obviously was important about this concession was that, while it had minimal public expenditure implications at the outset it accelerated the rate at which the costs of Britain's ageing population imposed heavy demands upon the Exchequer in the 1950s and 1960s.

Politically, the other interesting issue about the National Insurance Act concerns the determination of the levels of benefit. There was a continuing line of rhetoric, from the Beveridge Report through the statements made by Labour government spokesmen about the 'broad subsistence basis' for National Insurance (see discussion in Hess, 1981), that the scheme would largely eliminate the need for means-tested benefits. The latter were provided under another piece of legislation -the National Assistance Act of 1948 - which brought together in one scheme the responsibilities of the Assistance Board and the last vestiges of the cash-giving powers of the Poor Law. This measure provided benefits in 1948 only 2 shillings (5 pence, in modern currency) below the National Insurance rates for a single person or a married couple, but also added contributions towards rent (generally in full) on top of those allowances. Obviously, therefore, Beveridge's vision could only be readily realised by people with additional private resources and the National Assistance 'safety net' would not easily wither away.

Beveridge clearly recognised the significance of the 'problem of rent' but rejected the idea that there should be any special adjustments for it. As was commented in Chapter 2, Beveridge proceeded to adopt a harsh definition of subsistence levels. As Veit Wilson (1992) has shown, despite his fine rhetoric, Beveridge clearly let expediency - after advice from the Treasury - dictate his proposed benefit rates. Thereafter there was confusion about the distinction between subsistence levels as an overall issue and the matching of those levels to individual circumstances. The 1944 White Paper argued:

> In fixing the rates of benefit to be provided... the Government have considered whether it would be practicable to adopt a subsistence level of benefits... they expressed the preliminary view that it was not practical and further examination of the question has confirmed this view (HMSO, Cmd. 6550, 1944, para 12).

It then went on to refer explicitly to variations of costs between households, and in particular the issue of rent.

In his comments about the measure, including his second reading speech, Griffiths endorsed this view but at the same time reasserted the claim that the scheme had a broad subsistence basis. In presenting the National Assistance Bill to Parliament (Hansard Vol. 444, Session 1947-48) the Minister of Health, Aneurin Bevan, saw it as a scheme 'to assist people in peculiar and special circumstances' including some situations in which individuals would be ineligible for insurance benefits but not mentioning situations in which need might arise because those benefits were inadequate in amount. In summing up the debate, his National Insurance colleague, Mr Griffiths, did recognise this role for National Assistance, but was mainly concerned to stress how the National Insurance scheme would lift individuals off Assistance. In between these contributions no opposition or Labour backbench speaker suggested that there might be a problem about the relationship between the two schemes. The confused rhetoric of the time seemed to be closing the debate about the adequacy of the various benefit levels, and the relationships between them. In fact this was re-opened later to play a central role in the politics of social security from the 1960s onwards.

A related issue on which the politics of the 1940s seems, in retrospect, very naive concerns the uprating of benefits. At that time no specific provisions were made for revising either Insurance or Assistance rates as the cost of living rose. This oversight also implied a lack of thought about the movements of the two relative to each other. A concern to phase out Assistance should have implied a commitment to moving

Insurance rates up faster than Assistance ones. In fact what occurred caused the relationship to move in the opposite way. There were two upward adjustments to National Assistance rates in 1950 and 1951; pensions were only raised in 1951 and the other main insurance benefits were left untouched. Table 3.2 shows the benefit rates for married couples under both schemes after their introduction, after the 1950 changes to the Assistance rates and after the 1951 changes.

Table 3.2   *Married couples' insurance and assistance rates compared 1948-51*

Date	Assistance rate	Pensions rate	Short-term benefits rate
July 1948	£2.00	£2.10	£2.10
June 1950	£2.175	£2.10	£2.10
Sept 1951	£2.50	£2.50	£2.10

The government let the Assistance rate exceed the Insurance rates after the first change. Then the following year it moved up both the Assistance rate and the Insurance pension rate, and enabled the latter to catch up. However inaction on the other Insurance benefits meant that they were left even further behind the Assistance rate.

The Introduction of the National Health Service

The introduction of the health service has been the most studied of all the social policy innovations of the 1945-51 Government (Eckstein, 1958; Lindsey, 1962; Pater, 1981). It is seen as the central achievement of that Government and perhaps as the 'jewel in the crown' of the British welfare state. Its introduction was the responsibility of the most charismatic of British Labour politicians, the only modern British politician who has come close to being regarded as a socialist 'hero', Aneurin Bevan. But it has also been seen as a classic example of 'provider' capture of a service, for which the compliance of the doctors was bought at a very high price. As was suggested in the last chapter it is also another example of an innovation which was foreshadowed by extensive war-time developments.

From the time of the establishment of the social-insurance based medical service in 1911, blueprints had begun to be drawn up for an integrated medical service. A government commissioned report published in 1920, the Dawson Report, was the first major example. In the inter-war period the Socialist Medical Association had been a strong champion of a free public service and even the British Medical Association, the most obstructive actor in the battle described below, had argued in favour of extending the health insurance scheme. The war, as was pointed out in the last chapter, made some temporary integration of hospital services necessary. Finally, in the period of Coalition Government, a White Paper had been published proposing a scheme offering free services but with both general practitioners and voluntary hospitals enjoying considerable autonomy. There had been extensive negotiations with doctors and the other interested parties both before and after the publication of the White Paper.

Aneurin Bevan was determined to initiate the legislative process without being dragged into another round of negotiations. Foot suggests that this was a point of principle for him:

> No one in the previous Parliament had protested more vigorously than Bevan that precise negotiations with outside bodies about major legislative measures subverted the authority of the House of Commons (Foot, 1975, p.116).

That had not stopped Bevan from seeking allies informally and, in particular, from securing a measure of support from key leaders of the hospital doctors within the Royal Colleges. Nor, of course, did it prevent negotiations within the Government where a crucial issue about the role of local government had to be settled.

The National Health Service Bill was introduced into the House of Commons in March 1946. It started with clear assertions of the responsibility of central government for the health of the nation and of the principle that services should normally be free of charge. For the hospitals it proposed a system of direct control through Regional Hospital Boards responsible to the Minister, with Hospital Management Committees under them. It made medical teaching hospitals directly accountable to the Minister with special governing arrangements of their own. It provided for salaried hospital doctors, but allowed consultants to continue to treat private patients, and it offered a special system of 'merit awards' for the best consultants.

Bevan had abandoned Willink's attempt to appease both local authority interests and the voluntary hospitals by means of a loose structure under the coordination of joint boards of local authorities. He had to fight the strong local government interests within his own party on this; he experienced resistance from a senior minister, Herbert Morrison, who had been closely associated in the past with the government of London. Bevan insisted that there must be direct central government control. He also argued that the small size of many local authorities would make necessary the adoption of 'joint boards' which would not work very well and that his reform could not await the restructuring of local government. Under the proposals the higher-tier local authorities were left with responsibility for community health services - community nursing and health visiting, school health services and a general range of duties in respect of the protection of the public from environmental hazards.

The other important aspect of the proposals concerning the hospitals was the way in which the interests of the leading consultants were protected, with rights to continue private practice, merit awards and a special status for the high-prestige teaching hospitals. In later years a story circulated that Bevan boasted that he had secured the consultants' support for the scheme by 'stuffing their mouths with gold'.

Bevan's proposals for general practitioner services involved their operation under the surveillance of local committees (Executive Councils), with strong practitioner representation. Doctors were to be paid with a combination of a salary and a capitation fee (based upon the numbers of patients they took on). Their right to buy and sell practices was to be ended, though existing practitioners were to be compensated for the loss of this right. Doctor-dominated Medical Practice Committees were to control entry to new practices in order to deal with problems of maldistribution. A special tribunal was to be set up to deal with issues concerning breach of service contracts (discipline). A long-run aim was to establish health centres, owned by local authorities who would let accommodation to doctors.

The arrangements for general practice provoked the fiercest opposition to the legislation. Whilst the Conservatives took up the attack on the plan, the really important conflict occurred outside Parliament between Bevan and the doctors. The main source of debating material for Conservative opponents of the bill was the medical profession itself. A 'negotiating committee' was set up to deal with the health service plans; this represented both the British Medical Association (BMA) and the consultants' Royal Colleges, but the former was the dominant force. The BMA represented the profession as a whole, but was dominated by general practitioners. It was an unwieldy organisation with a complex democratic structure. The regular meetings of its 70 person Council tended to be dominated by a vociferous minority who were very hostile to state medicine (see Foot, 1975, pp.113-16; also Eckstein, 1960). This Council came out strongly against the bill, objecting particularly to the abolition of the sale of practices, to the tribunal proposed for disciplinary purposes and, above all, to the threat of a salaried service for which the proposal for a part-salary (of £300) alongside capitation was seen as the thin end of the wedge.

As the Bill went through Parliament, Bevan's relationship with the doctors entered a confused phase in which 'negotiations' were attempted. As far as Bevan was concerned these were to be merely about details, whereas the doctors' aim was to throw out much of the legislation. Meanwhile Bevan had to satisfy his own backbench supporters that he was giving nothing away. Symptomatic of this problem was the obvious desire of the Labour Left that further evolution to a salaried medical service should occur. During the second reading debate, Bevan had said he did not think the medical profession was 'ripe for this' and then subsequently added 'There is all the difference between plucking fruit when it is ripe and plucking it when it is green' (Foot, 1975, p.151). Overall there was a strong tendency for Bevan's opponents, both in the medical profession and in Parliament, to characterise him, on the strength of his earlier political record, as a dogmatic socialist determined to accrue centralised power to himself and his ministry. Indiscretions like the one quoted above did not reassure them.

The new service was due to start on 5 July 1948. By the beginning of that year the BMA's stance had become so intransigent that the Government took the unusual step of staging a Parliamentary debate reaffirming its commitment to the Act. Around the same time the results of a BMA plebiscite showed 40,814 doctors against the Act and only 4734 in support. It seemed likely that large numbers of doctors would refuse to join the service. Then Lord Moran, of the Royal College of Physicians, who had been willing to support Bevan from early on, came up with a compromise suggestion. He suggested that Bevan should agree to introduce an amending Act which stated clearly that no plan existed to introduce a salaried service for general practitioners, and that the £300 payment would be phased out. Bevan agreed to do this. The BMA leadership continued its hostility and attempted to reinforce its position with another plebiscite. This resulted in only a comparatively small majority against. What is more, the BMA Council had earlier said that it would advise against entering the service if the majority against included 13,000 general practitioners. It did not. Finally, while the BMA's leadership was still trying to make up its mind what to do, general practitioners starting enroling in considerable numbers to join the service on 5 July. The BMA gave in.

Hence, while it can be said that Bevan introduced a more unified and centralised service than that planned by Willink and that he pursued his plan with great determination against substantial medical opposition, it can equally be said that from the outset the National Health Service proposal was exceptionally deferential to medical interests and could only be implemented by a further concession to medical power. Whilst a ritual party battle was fought over the Act, the real politics of this policy involved an elaborate contest between the government and the doctors.

The governing structure adopted for the National Health Service involved central control, accompanied by arrangements for medical interests to be represented at all levels: in the Regional Hospital Boards and Hospital Management Committees, in the Executive Councils and related Medical Practices Committees and even inside the Ministry of Health. An alternative model for governing the service through local government was rejected, with local authorities being compensated by opportunities to be represented within the governing bodies. This was one of the few changes from the Willink plan which did please the doctors. There are good reasons to accept Bevan's view that the local government structure of the day was not very appropriate (with too many small authorities even in the upper tier) for the management of this new service. However, in the long run this choice had important implications for limiting consumer influence upon this centralised and provider dominated service.

It is interesting to note that the Willink plan would have enabled many of the old voluntary hospitals to operate as 'contractors' to the health service. Bevan insisted upon a more unified structure. He was strongly criticised by the Conservatives for this. The wheel was eventually to turn almost full circle in the 1980s when the Thatcher government provided hospitals and other health care providers with the opportunity to become self-governing trusts. Many of the hospitals whose historical roots were in the old voluntary sector were amongst the earliest units to bid for this form of quasi-independence.

Housing Policy

Under the administrative arrangements of the era, housing policy was also the responsibility of the Ministry of Health until 1951 when it was transferred to the new Ministry of Local Government and Planning. Attention is being given briefly here to this other area of Aneurin Bevan's responsibilities (until he was moved to the Ministry of Labour in January

1951) because of some interesting features of the politics of what would seem on the surface to be an uncomplicated area of public policy but which proved to be difficult for the 1945-51 government.

In its manifesto the Labour Party said:

> Housing will be one of the greatest and one of the earlier tests of a Government's real determination to put the nation first. Labour's pledge is firm and direct - it will proceed with a housing programme with the maximum practical speed until every family in this island has a good standard of accommodation.

Labour left itself very open to attack on this issue, and it will be seen, in the next chapter, how much of this job was left for further dynamic action by the Conservatives. There are lessons here on some of the more complex aspects of the politics of social policy.

Again, there was complete two party agreement about the need to initiate substantial house building programme after the years of neglect during the war. But the size of the problem was underestimated, not least by the Ministry itself; it quoted 750,000 as a target to put things right whereas the need was very much greater than that. Then, to make things worse, it proved very difficult to accelerate the house building programme, first because of a lack of skilled manpower and, second, a lack of materials. The first problem was exacerbated by the government's commitment to an orderly process of demobilisation after the war. The second was a product of the serious run down of domestic enterprise as a whole and of the war indebtedness and balance of payments crisis which restricted the import of materials. In 1946 the government was embarrassed by a squatting campaign (Sissons and French, 1963, pp. 43-6). Once the programme got started it was afflicted by the economic problems which emerged during the winter of 1946-47. The overall house-building performance during the years 1945-51 is set out in table 3.3.

Bevan, as a Left Wing Minister who had been a severe critic of the Coalition during the war, was identified as a particular target for attack by the Opposition (see Foot, 1975, Chapter 2). His performance on housing was savaged, and the Conservatives set out to make house building one of their prime social policy achievements in the 1950s. Quite apart from his difficulties in getting the programme going, Bevan's housing policy had two characteristics which were attacked by the Conservatives. One of them was Bevan's insistence that local authorities letting houses to people in need should be the dominant house providers, as opposed to speculative builders producing houses for sale. The former should be enabled to do this with the help of significantly increased subsidies (compared to pre-war levels) from central government.

Table 3.3   *House completions 1945-51 (thousands)*

	By local authorities	By private builders	By others	Total
1945	1	-	-	1
1946	21	30	-	51
1947	87	40	1	128
1948	171	31	5	206
1949	142	25	5	172
1950	139	27	7	172
1951	142	21	9	172

Source: Ministry of Housing and Local Government, *Housing Returns for England and Wales*, quoted in Donnison, 1960

The other feature of Bevan's approach was his insistence upon comparatively high standards for council houses (a space standard of 900 square feet as opposed to the pre-war standard of 750 square feet). Bevan in fact had a vision of council housing as a provision for *all*. In the 1949 Housing Act he repealed the earlier provision that this should be 'housing for the working classes'. He had a poetic vision of unsegregated classless housing:

> We should try to introduce in our modern villages and towns what was always the lovely feature of English and Welsh villages, where the doctor, the grocer, the butcher and the farm labourer all lived in the same street. I believe that it is essential for the full life of a citizen... to see the living tapestry of a mixed community (Foot, 1975, p.76).

Here, then, was an attitudes which must inevitably have retarded the housing programme in quantitative terms, though justified as far as Bevan was concerned by a wider vision. This attitude opened up an ideological divide between Bevan and the Conservatives and, it must be said, between Bevan and some of his colleagues - the upper-class Dalton ridiculed him as a 'tremendous Tory' for insisting on quality in council house building! (Dalton, 1962, p.358). In fact, in his own brief period with responsibility for housing in 1951, Dalton initiated plans to reduce standards which were taken up by his Conservative successor (Seldon, 1981, p.254).

Looking back now there is a major contrast, still visible because houses last so long, between the high-quality council houses of the 1940s and the large housing output of the 1950s of both lower-quality public housing and vast estates of cheap owner-occupied houses. Bevan's vision was not sustained; class and housing quality are sharply correlated and British communities are fundamentally socially segregated. Was Bevan's vision ever sustainable? Or were the commercial and social pressures towards a segregated system, already manifesting themselves in the 1930s, too strong?

The 1945-51 Governments and the Personal Social Services

This section deals with an area of policy scarcely identified as needing attention in the Labour manifesto - the personal social services. It is an area of policy which, at that time, was not identified as a distinct sector of activity. It was also an area which was then largely unpoliticised; even today party battle lines are rarely clearly drawn up. In the 1940s some important innovations occurred which received very little political or public attention.

Neither of the major historical accounts of the 1945-51 Governments (Morgan, 1984, and Pelling, 1984) mentions the Children Act of 1948 and both confine their comments on the National Assistance Act to its provisions dealing with social security. Yet these two pieces of legislation, plus a part of the National Health Service Act that also attracted little attention (that part dealing with local authority health services) laid the foundations for the development of personal social services policy in Britain. Whilst the lack of attention to them reflects the politically uncontroversial nature of this legislation, the decisions of this period set up a series of dynamic processes, as they were implemented, which were important for the future politics of social policy. Both of these issues will be explored briefly.

The Children Act was a direct consequence of a sequence of events starting from a child care scandal during the war. A child, Denis O'Neill, was killed by his foster father in 1945. An enquiry into his death (the Monckton Enquiry, 1945) found that the existing legislation did not define a clear division of responsibility between the education authorities and the Poor Law. As a response to this, the Government set up a wider investigation into the services for deprived and neglected children (Curtis Committee, 1946). This recommended that there should be set up within each top-tier local authority a Children Committee with its own chief officer and trained staff. It should be the duty of this committee and department to investigate cases of child neglect and to take formal steps to bring children in need of protection into the care of the local authority.

Here then was a specific proposal to deal with most of the residual parts of the Poor Law concerned with children. The Children Act of 1948 enacted these recommendations. In doing so the government placed central responsibility for children's services with the Home Office. It has been suggested that it did this to try to ensure that this area of policy would get single minded attention. It might not have secured this within its obvious alternative bases at that time, education and health departments. Certainly the Ministry of Health made a bid for it (Means and Smith, 1985, p.135).

With a set of specific proposals in mind for children, the other welfare service part of the dismantled Poor Law for which a 'home' was needed was services to elderly and handicapped people. This is where the National Assistance Act was important. This also made the top tier of local government the responsible authority. However, the very specific proposal for children seems to have led the government to rule out the idea of a combined welfare department. In any case, as Means and Smith show, the Government's view of its aims here was the very limited one of transferring residential care. Certainly the Government saw itself as replacing old residential institutions by modern residential homes for which people would get benefits towards the 'rent' (plus pocket money). 'Old folks hotels' the media christened them (ibid., p.152). There was very little consideration at this time of the development of domiciliary services. The Ministry of Health failed to persuade the Treasury to allow local authorities a specific grant for this service, but after negotiation it did secure capital grants towards the development of new institutions.

However the National Health Act is relevant since this made the local authorities responsible for the development of community health services, including home help services. Some local authorities saw the health/social welfare connection and set up combined 'health and welfare departments'.

Looking to the future, this legislation had in practice set up three alternative but interrelated channels for local policy development (through children's, welfare and community health services). These offered a structure which would influence local initiatives in the implementation of a policy which was set out only in very general terms. The weakest of these, as writers like Townsend showed powerfully in the 1960s (Townsend, 1964) was the National Assistance Act, authorising the development of an institutional response to care needs. A long while later, this was one which ran into difficulties as a private but often social security subsidised sector developed alongside it (see Chapter 8). The health service legislation on the other hand, stimulated a range of domiciliary alternatives which were subsequently to be very important. It is interesting to note here how home help services established under this legislation, principally to meet the needs of new mothers in an era when home confinements were the norm, subsequently became a key element in the provision of home care for elderly people.

Alongside these health and welfare developments, the Children Act, with its demand for trained specialist staff, played an important role in the development of a new public service profession - social work. Packman has shown how the staff of the Children's Departments soon became important initiators of new approaches to their task, stressing the need for 'preventative' work alongside their powers to take children into care. Eventually they played a key role in the development of integrated 'social services departments' to take on generic responsibilities in the personal social services (Packman, 1975).

There was thus a contrast at the local level between a rather muddled package of general community health and welfare measures and new departments set up with a clear 'mission' under the Children Act. Griffith (1966) has shown how this difference was reinforced by the much clearer central inspection system set up for the latter, pushing standards forward and guaranteeing a dialogue between local and central government. The final advantage for the children service was that responsibility for it was placed in a high prestige ministry (the Home Office) rather than in the Department of Health.

Education: Implementing the 1944 Act

On education policy, Labour's 1945 election manifesto merely said:

> An important step forward has been taken by the passing of the recent Education Act. Labour will put that Act not merely into legal force but into practical effect, including the raising of the school leaving age to 16 at the earliest possible moment...

Similarly the 1950 manifesto merely boasted about the raising of the school leaving age (not mentioning of course that it merely raised it to 15 - as embodied in the 1944 Act. The raising of the age to 16 was in the end, an unachieved objective of the 1964-70 Labour government, see Chapter 5). It also drew attention to the fact that new schools were being built.

Hence, in these policy statements, no attention was devoted to the education issue which was soon to become so important for the Labour Party - the establishment, within the framework of the 1944 Act, of a comprehensive rather than a selective system of secondary education. Morgan (1984, pp.177-8) reports that the Labour party rank and file was restless about this almost from the outset of the government. The National Association of Labour Teachers was arguing for the development of comprehensive schools, and its case was taken up by a number of backbench MPs. But it was not until 1950 that the party's National Executive was even willing to set up a working party on the subject. A few Labour-controlled local authorities (notably the London and West Riding County Councils) pushed forward schemes, embodied in their building plans, but the Ministry was unwilling to consider schemes not founded upon the development of new and large schools (Benn and Simon, 1972, pp.43-5).

Morgan (1984) sees Labour's education achievements as providing an initial impetus towards educational expansion, allowing both for the extra year and for the first post-war 'baby boom' generation. But he draws attention to the deep conservatism of the Labour leadership (itself a contrasting combination of Public School products and other members, most of whom had succeeded in the working-class movement despite a minimum of formal education). He argues:

> the way was paved for the education boom of the fifties and sixties, although on the basis of a structure of secondary and higher education which offered little intellectual innovation or social inter-mingling (Morgan, 1984, p.179).

Rearmament and the Social Policy Budget 1950-51

In the first years of the National Health Service it was found that costs were growing rapidly and surpassing the sums 'voted' for the service. In the incomplete financial year from its inception in July 1948 to the following March, it cost 251.2 million pounds as opposed to the 241.4 millions anticipated. If those figures are translated to full-year equivalents they would amount to 339.6 million pounds as against 326.3 million. In the next year (1949-50) the estimate was put up to 387.6 million pounds and expenditure remained just within it. But in 1950-51 the annual cost was 405.8 million pounds against an estimate of 398.3 million (Guillebaud Report, 1956, p.7). Of course those figures ignore inflation, but it was at a rate of only about 3 per cent per annum at that time. Taking inflation into account suggests that the real cost growth rate was around 6 per cent per annum, using the 1948-49 actual figure rather than the estimate as a base line. Comparison with figures given in later chapters suggests that this was a strong but not exceptional growth rate. The problem at the time seemed to have been a naive expectation that, with better services available, demand would fall as sickness was cured more effectively.

The Cabinet seems to have reacted strongly even to the initial divergence between the estimate and the actual cost. As early as October 1949 the Chancellor of the Exchequer, Stafford Cripps, sought to get Aneurin Bevan to agree to the imposition of prescription charges. Bevan accepted this only 'in principle'. Next spring Cripps tried again, this time seeking charges for dentures, spectacles and appliances. Bevan again resisted, fiercely defending the principle of a free health service (see Morgan, 1984, pp.412-13), but agreed upon the careful monitoring of health service costs.

Two developments then occurred. In October the ailing Cripps was replaced as Chancellor by Hugh Gaitskell. Bevan was never close to Gaitskell and resented his rapid rise. He, by contrast, was moved laterally to the Ministry of Labour in January 1951. Hence, there was potential for a personality clash, something not to be underrated in political explanations (see also Morgan, 1992, p.163).

The second development was the intensification of the Korean War, which had started in June 1950. Britain supported the United States but was apprehensive about any escalation of the conflict. From Kenneth Morgan's account of these events is quite clear that the United States extracted a price from its restraining ally - a substantial increase in defence expenditure and the extension of national military service from one and a half to two years. In January 1951 it was agreed that British defence expenditure would go up to 4,700 million pounds over the three years 1951-54. It had dropped as low as 750 million by the beginning of 1950. It never went as high as those planned figures; significantly the incoming Conservative Government curbed its growth, but that is beside the point here.

In order to provide for this expenditure growth, Hugh Gaitskell proposed some health expenditure cuts and the imposition of charges for dentures, spectacles and prescriptions. The Cabinet accepted the first two but rejected prescription charges. Bevan, another Cabinet Minister (Harold Wilson) and a junior minister (John Freeman) resigned. Their arguments, set out in various ways at the time and since, rested on a combination of objections to the attack on the principles of a free health service and on the size of the increases in the defence budget. This was a crucial conflict contributing to the decline and fall of the Labour administration. This story has been recounted here because it is the first time in which, during the period covered by this book, social policy expenditure control surfaced as central to a government's debate about its budget. Kenneth Morgan, in telling the story, seems fairly convinced that it was a 'tragedy' which could have been avoided, rooted both in the political ambitions of the two main protagonists and in the Labour government's over-reaction to the escalation of the 'cold war'. In many ways the health service charges were symbolic: they did little to restrain demand (indeed they initially escalated demand as people sought attention before the charges were imposed) and they contributed little to the budget. Yet this incident is the first of many in the recent history of social policy in which a government's desire to continue to play a decisive role in the world and its reluctance to raise public expenditure combined to create problems for social policy. It is a dramatic demonstration of the inter-connectedness of public policy, which makes it impossible to make a case for social policy expenditure without at the same time countering the arguments in support of other policies.

Conclusions

The Government of 1945-51 enacted a range of social policy measures, most of which were anticipated in its manifesto and which had been the subject of preparatory work during the Coalition Government. The Conservative manifesto contained a similar programme, and in one respect - housing - that party's criticisms of Labour from the opposition benches consisted primarily of indicating that it could have done better. The new National Insurance system was introduced in an apparent atmosphere of consensus, with the parameters of that consensus laid down by the Treasury before Labour came to power.

The only social policy legislation over which the parties seemed to be involved in sharp conflict was the National Health Service Act. On this the Conservatives largely took their lead from the doctors, suggesting that they could have offered the country a health service which was less centralised and in which less control was exercised over doctors' primary care practices.

Otherwise the opposition concentrated its attacks upon the Labour government on its economic rather than its social policies, and particularly on nationalisation. It is a futile exercise in speculative alternative history to try to judge whether the Conservatives, in the face of the many economic difficulties of the post-war period, would have pursued social policy goals as single-mindedly as Labour did in its first three years of office. But Labour's determination despite those difficulties should not be underestimated. It provides a dramatic contrast with the post-First World War period when Lloyd George turned sharply away from social expenditure in the middle of his term of office.

It has been shown that at the outset Labour had to secure a loan from the United States to prevent the national indebtedness problem from overwhelming all its plans, but that then it proceeded single-mindedly with its social programme without worrying much about its cost. The demobilisation programme helped by rapidly reducing public expenditure on defence. The social security legislation had been costed earlier, during the preparation of and early debates about the Beveridge Report and for the 1944 White Paper. In a way which has since been abandoned in government financial planning, the social security scheme was seen as largely self-funded because insurance contributions would make a significant addition to government income to pay for it. The cost of the National Health Service was underestimated. The Government had rejected using more than a small part of the insurance contribution as a source of funds for the health service. It seems to have been optimistic about its capacity to limit health service costs without the imposition of controls or charges, on the grounds that a service which improved the health of the nation would have a consequent limiting impact on the demands on itself. When it found that, on the contrary, demand was rising sharply it began to worry about health service costs (around the end of 1949). Then, in 1950-51 the cost of rearmament was responsible for initiating a conflict within the government about health policy cost control.

Labour feared that unemployment would be a crucial social policy issue. The government was very committed to the prevention of a rise in unemployment. It expected that the country would experience a post-war recession like that encountered after the First World War (see Cairncross, 1985, chapter 14), and for these reasons it attempted to engage in manpower planning. But apart from a worrying spell early in 1947, when a fuel supply crisis combined with bad weather to push unemployment up sharply, the government did not really have to engage with this issue in any way which requires exploration in this account of the politics of social policy. The American commitment to stable international trade and European recovery was clearly important in avoiding a repetition of the problems which followed the First World War. Subsequently rearmament may have helped to continue the growth started by steady post-war recovery, but the impact of this lies primarily outside the period with which this chapter is concerned.

This, then, has been an account of social policy growth in a context of relative political consensus. Much of the politics described was not so much struggles within Parliament between the parties as conflicts over departmental and professional interests. The battles between Bevan and the doctors and the struggles within the government itself over health service charges were the most significant examples of this. The overall mood of consensus continued into the years of the next government, as will be seen in the next chapter.

4   The Conservative Governments 1951-64

Introduction

The fall of Labour from government in 1951 marked the start of 13 years of Conservative rule. The Conservatives won a narrow majority in 1951 on a lower overall poll than Labour. They gained 321 seats to Labour's 295. There were only 9 other members, the 1950s being an era in which the political contest was very clearly a straight fight between the two main parties. The Conservative share of the vote was 48.0 per cent, Labour received 48.8 per cent.

In the subsequent elections of 1955 and 1959 the Conservatives strengthened their hold on power. Their numbers went up to 344 out of 630 in 1955 and to 365 in 1959. In these two elections they received very nearly 50 per cent of the votes cast and were comfortably ahead of Labour.

The Conservatives were led, over this period, by four different Prime Ministers: Winston Churchill, the ageing leader of the war-time coalition, from 1951 to 1955; Anthony Eden from 1955 to the beginning of 1957; Harold Macmillan from 1957 to 1963 and Sir Alec Douglas-Home for their final year in office.

Despite the fact that there were three Parliaments and four Prime Ministers over this period, this chapter will deal with these years of Conservative rule as a whole. It was not an era of significant social policy change. What is remarkable about it, at least when viewed from the far side of the experience of Conservative rule in the 1980s, is the extent to which it was a period of continuity for social policy. The Conservatives did little to undo the structure of social policy created by Labour; rather they concentrated on managing its development or at least upon maintaining the status quo.

A crucial initial task for this chapter, therefore, is to explain this continuity. Conservative rhetoric at this time suggests that many leading members of the party had doubts about the 'welfare state'. As early as 1950 a group of younger Conservatives published a pamphlet in which, whilst endorsing the general case for social policy, they suggested that the egalitarian and universalist thrust of Labour policies had gone too far (Macleod and Maude, 1950). In 1955 the Institute of Economic Affairs was founded, and started to produce a stream of pamphlets advocating increased selectivity and greater use of market principles in social policy. The issue of the cost of the welfare state and its implications both for economic management and for the Conservative aspiration to cut taxes had already been put on the political agenda before the fall of Labour. The Treasury kept that concern on the agenda throughout the early 1950s (see Howard on Butler as Chancellor of the Exchequer, 1987; and Lowe, 1989). At the beginning of 1958 a Chancellor of the Exchequer, Peter Thorneycroft, resigned after failing to secure Cabinet agreement for a package of public expenditure cuts which included the withdrawal of family allowances for the second child and hospital boarding charges.

In explaining why reaction against the welfare state made so little impact there is a need to look at the perspectives of some of the key politicians and at the Conservative view of the electoral strategy necessary to keep them in power. There is also a need to examine what was happening to the economy and the overall pattern of public expenditure and taxation, and to ask questions about the strength of the pressures upon the government from the likely advocates of reaction. Finally, it is important to raise some questions about the character of the relationships between politicians and public servants during this period.

Over a period of 13 years the party political personnel changed dramatically. At the beginning a 77-year old Winston Churchill formed a government in which many of his old war-time colleagues took the senior posts. Churchill himself, despite a capacity to make vituperative party political speeches at times, was in many respects a consensus figure. He was proud of having led a coalition government in the war. He had also one of the architects of the Liberal social programme in the period before the First World War. In his last period in office he gave little attention to domestic policies;, he was principally concerned to try to continue to play his role as an international statesman. Nevertheless he was proud to proclaim in 1954:

> We have improved all the social services and we are spending more this year
> on them than any Government at any time (speech in May 1954, quoted in
> Seldon, 1981, pp.244-5).

Churchill's successor, Anthony Eden, had little interest in domestic politics, and soon became embroiled in the Suez 'adventure' which brought about his downfall. The crucial Premier as far as social policy was concerned was Harold Macmillan. He had been on the Tory Left in the 1930s, deeply critical of his party's record on unemployment. On that issue he said, in 1958:

> I am determined, as far as it lies within human power, never to let this shadow fall again upon our country (Macmillan, quoted in Raison, 1990).

Macmillan's only significant experience as a departmental minister, moreover, was as the leader of the great house-building drive in the early 1950s, on which more will be said later. The Macmillan governments, naturally, brought more of the younger Tories into high office. Yet, as above-mentioned clash with Thorneycroft illustrates, there was a tendency for the centrists to dominate. In some cases - the extreme example is Sir Edward Boyle, who became Minister of Education in 1962 - some Left-wing Tories became influential.

The other key figure in domestic politics over almost the whole of this period was R.A. Butler. Despite the fact that he was the exponent of a tough Treasury line against public expenditure as Chancellor of the Exchequer from 1951 to 1955, he had been the progenitor of the 1944 Education Act and the key figure in the modernisation of the Tory party during its period in opposition. Towards the end of his political career, from 1957 to 1962, he was a comparatively liberal leader of that most illiberal of government departments, the Home Office. Overall he was a moderating and cautious influence upon his party.

Macmillan's forthright statement about unemployment, which rings a surprising note after a decade of Thatcherism, was in many respects a reflection of the consensus view in 1958. Furthermore the Conservatives came to believe that neglecting to maintain full employment would lose them an election. Similarly, they came to accept that both the national health service and state pensions policy were important for the electorate. They also considered that their attack upon Labour for its inadequate housing drive had helped them to win the 1951 election.

It has already been suggested that a central theme throughout the period covered by this book is the conflict between three concerns: sustaining a strong economy, maintaining a world power role for Britain and the meeting the needs of the welfare state. For much of the period 1951 to 1964 there were factors which prevented this conflict from coming to a head. The economy was growing and sustaining full employment. The fact that this growth rate was inferior to that of competitor powers only really began to emerge as an issue for the balance of payments and the exchange rate towards the end of the period. Labour's 1949 devaluation had staved off the latter problem for a while, and after the dislocation of the war the issues about differential growth rates only slowly got on the agenda. The 'peace dividend' from defence expenditure continued to be realised to some extent; indeed Macmillan regarded the continuation of Britain's role as a nuclear power as necessary to curb expenditure on conventional forces by abolishing national service (Horne, 1989, vol. 2, pp.50-51).

Over the whole period 1951 to 1964 social expenditure grew at a little over 4 per cent per annum. The highest rates of increase were in education, at 5.6 per cent, and social security, at 4.9 per cent. The rate of increase for health and personal social services expenditure was 3.1 per cent and for housing 2.5 per cent (Walker, ed., 1982, p.30). Over the same period the share of public expenditure taken by defence fell from 9.1 per cent to 6.7 per cent, even though the actual amount of defence expenditure expanded slightly in real (as opposed to merely 'money') terms. But it was social expenditure growth which significantly pushed up public expenditure as a whole.

Whilst it will be seen that these growth rates were exceeded by the succeeding Labour government and by Heath's Conservative government, they did exceed the expenditure growth rates recorded since 1975. It is interesting to note the education expenditure growth rate was well above that for health - evidence that the demographic pressure on expenditure in this period came more from the beginning than the end of the life cycle.

Social expenditure growth exceeded that of the Gross Domestic Product over this period. The latter was 2.8 per cent per annum. Hence the social expenditure share of GDP rose from 16.1 per cent in 1951 to 19.3 per cent in 1964 (ibid., p.28).

The two great sources of social expenditure growth over the post-war period as a whole - health and pensions costs - began to cause concern over this period, even though the consequences of an ageing population were only just beginning to be realised. The key enquiry into health costs, the Guillebaud Report (1956), concluded that there was no great cause for alarm (see later section). There also seemed to be scope for new policies to deal with the pensions cost problem (see below).

Hence, although at the beginning of the 13-year period the growth of public expenditure relative to GDP began to give cause for anxiety, economic growth in the middle 1950s reassured the government on that point. At the end of that decade Macmillan was able to preside cheerfully over a country where both private incomes and public sector expenditures were growing. The 1959 election occurred at the high point of this conjunction, with an inflationary pre-election budget to reinforce the impression of prosperity. Macmillan was willing to take risks with inflation. The consequences of those risks began to become apparent in the early 1960s, it was then that the rate of growth of public expenditure again began to surge ahead of the economic growth rate.

The Conservatives put income tax up a little in the anxious period after 1951, but then implemented a series of downward adjustments through the rest of their period of rule. Growth plus inflation yielded more government income despite this.

Overall, it is suggested that there are a number of reasons why the Conservatives did not come under irresistible pressure from the advocates of reductions in social expenditure during this period. The economy was growing, tax rates were falling and, whilst the stop/go processes of post-Keynesian economic management were causing problems (see Brittan, 1971), there was as yet no mood of 'crisis'. Attacks on public expenditure were repulsed with arguments about the contribution the 'social wage' provided to keeping cash wages down (Lowe, 1989) and to the maintenance of industrial peace.

The Conservative ministers with direct responsibility for social policy in this period concentrated upon being good managers of the welfare state. This is the era in which two cherished myths of political science (which were partly refuted in the 1980s) came to be established. One of these was that spending department ministers would, regardless of ideology, tend to be the advocates of growth in their own budgets (see Heclo and Wildavsky, 1981, pp.134-51). The other was that ministers would always tend to be weak influences upon departmental policies, since they would be likely to be temporary visitors lacking in expertise in comparison to permanent civil servants (Blondel, 1963, pp.156-8).

The second point is worth a little further comment. Over this period in each of the three ministries of housing, education and pensions there were five different ministers. Health had eight ministers in all over the period. Only the ministry of housing was consistently represented in the Cabinet, and the pensions ministry (which was not combined with national insurance until 1953) scarcely ever had its political head in the Cabinet. This was still the era when social policy was outside the range of issues which the Conservative leadership regarded as the concerns of 'high politics' (Kavanagh, 1990, p.284). It was a time when younger politicians like Iain Mcleod could be appointed to the Ministry of Health with very little political experience (Fisher, 1973). It is perhaps not surprising that this was a period when ministers were dominated by civil servants. In the following sections of this chapter, dealing with key issues in social policy, the theme of civil servant domination and of the importance of professional interests and professionally inspired initiatives will be explored further.

Housing - An Emphasis upon Quantity but not Quality

Although crucial for the electoral politics of 1950-51, housing policy in this era was very much a matter of administration rather than politics. The political commitment to the housing drive left the new Minister of Housing, Harold Macmillan, in a strong position to make demands for subsidies and for the relaxation of capital spending controls, against Treasury opposition. Housing investment moreover received higher priority than health and education expenditure in the early 1950s.

The housing drive was a great success. It started with a continued emphasis upon the public sector, then this was gradually shifted towards the owner-occupied sector (where direct public subsidy - as opposed to tax relief - was not involved). The record is set out in Table 4.1, with the period of earlier Labour rule included for comparison.

Table 4.1   House Completions 1945-64 (annual averages - thousands)

	Public sector	Private sector	Total
1945-51	113	28	141
1951-55	224	67	291
1956-59	159	135	294
1960-64	137	186	322

Source Ministry of Housing and Local Government, *Housing Returns for England and Wales* various dates

Macmillan got much of the credit for starting initiating this drive. He moved on to higher office in 1954 and was Prime Minister by 1957.

However, this success was bought at a price. The large quantitative output was secured partly by lowering standards. By the early 1990s some of the public sector houses built during this era have deteriorated or become so unpopular that they are unlettable. A particular problem sector has been high-rise houses. These were generally built by using industrial processes, involving the pre-casting of concrete pieces away from the site. The special politics of this development have been examined by Dunleavy (1981). He has uncovered an unsavoury combination of high pressure salesmanship, professionals determined that they knew best and not a little corruption. It comprised a comparatively private politics of influence upon administration within local authorities, of both political persuasions, with the active support of central government. It occurred during the last years of Conservative rule in the 1960s and the first years of the subsequent Labour regime. Between 1956 and 1967 flats in high-rise blocks attracted additional government subsidy, resulting in rapidly increased output after 1956, as Table 4.2 shows.

Table 4.2   Development of High-rise Flats

Years	Number (thousands)
1953-55	24
1956-58	29
1959-61	48
1962-64	82
1965-67	118
1968-70	55
1971-73	17

Source: Statistics taken from tender approval data quoted in Dunleavy, 1981.

A rather similar private politics applied to the development of slum clearance policies during this period. As the housing boom proceeded, waiting lists for council houses began to shorten. Administrative statistics of this kind need interpreting with caution; at best they only measure needs as defined by providers. However, the official view was that this fall in waiting lists meant that policy should shift to give more attention to the replacement of unsatisfactory houses. Government subsidy policies were altered to increase the sums available for pulling down unfit houses

and rehousing their occupants. Two characteristics of this policy came under attack: first, the extent to which clearance was being undertaken when renovation was still a possibility and, second, the tendency to decant communities to other areas rather than to reconstruct the neighbourhoods where they already lived. Obviously these two characteristics were linked. The expression 'private politics' was used in relation to slum clearance for several reasons: (1) because there was little disagreement between the political parties on this development; (2) because the most visible policy-makers were planners and housing officials whom Davies portrayed as 'evangelistic bureaucrats' (Davies, 1974); and (3) because a range of rather less visible development industry interests stood to gain from the releasing of inner urban sites. Again this development spanned the later Conservative years and the era of Labour rule in the 1960s. Significant documentation of the process by Dennis (1970 and 1972) and by Davies (1974) pertains to the later period. Nevertheless one of the earliest attacks on the breaking up of communities in this way was a book published by Michael Young and Peter Wilmot as far back as 1957. It took the 'policy community' a long while to pay attention!

The Conservatives made it very clear, in their attacks on Labour's housing policy and in their own electoral programmes, that they wanted to encourage owner-occupation. It has already been shown how they encouraged a shift from public to private housing investment. But the development of the owner-occupied sector clearly depended upon something more than government policy alone. It grew in size in the 1950s as individual incomes increased as a result of the restoration of peace-time economic conditions accompanied by full employment. It was assisted by the readiness of the building industry to provide cheap houses for sale and by the growth of the building societies as sources of loans (see Boddy, 1980).

Then, at the end of the period of Conservative rule, the private sector received a further stimulus from public policy. Purchasers of houses had been able to secure tax relief on mortgage interest payments because the were required to pay a tax on the notional value of their asset known ; 'schedule A tax'. This was a logical connection, as it would have be unjust to be taxing an asset which, because of a mortgage, was not fu realisable. But that logical connection was severed in 1963 w' schedule A tax was abolished but the accompanying tax relief was r

Thus a substantial subsidy to owner-occupation was created. Ir debate on the 1963 budget the opposition warmly welcomed the abo' of schedule A tax. The only hint of awareness of the implications measure was a speech by Douglas Houghton from the oppositio

which dealt with the absence of any comparable help for rent payers. Houghton, a former income tax official said that it 'flies in the face of more than one Royal Commission though that does not prove it wrong. Right or wrong it is welcome to six and a quarter million owner-occupiers but there are over nine million tenants' (Hansard, 1962-63, Vol. 675, col. 1113). Houghton must have had in mind the 1955 Royal Commission on Taxation of Profits and Income which recommended the retention of schedule A tax in the interest of equity between owners and tenants (see Boddy, 1980, p.133). Hence, though there was some awareness of the subsidy to owner-occupiers there was a willingness, on all sides, to turn a blind eye to any wider implications or consequences, in the interests of giving a benefit to owner-occupiers. Houghton asked, 'Can we regard £48 million of revenue as the price for recovering Orpington?' (Hansard, 1962-63, Vol. 675, col. 1113). He was referring to a Conservative Parliamentary seat recently lost to the Liberals.

Boddy points out that the yield of schedule A would have risen significantly from the comparatively low figure of the time (Boddy, 1980, p.133), but even more significant was the rise in the value of the concession embodied in tax relief on mortgage interest as both prices and interest rates rose. This was to play a key role in the future growth of owner-occupation, and to come under attack as a relatively uncontrollable and illogical public subsidy which tended to advantage the most prosperous buyers and have a perverse effect on the rise of house prices. Future governments of both parties were from time to time embarrassed by it, yet nervous of the electoral consequences of a direct attack upon it.

Whilst the encouragement of the owner-occupied sector was the main way in which the Conservatives stimulated the development of the private sector in housing, the partial elimination of the crisis of acute housing undersupply by the mid-1950s led the government to see whether it could restore the private rented market, largely controlled since 1916 and heavily controlled since the Second World War. An Act passed in 1957 allowed for gradual decontrol, whilst protecting sitting tenants. At the end of the period of Conservative rule, that measure was seen as contributing to the development of an unsavoury and aggressive form of private landlordism, called 'Rachmanism' after one of its most unscrupulous practitioners. This was principally a London problem, and it is debatable to what extent the objective of this activity was the replacement of controlled tenancies by uncontrolled ones as opposed to driving out tenants in order to sell properties. Clearly, however, selective as opposed to general rent restriction policies left scope for activities designed to evade control. This aspect of Conservative policy had a more distinctive

ideological hallmark than most of the other policies discussed in this chapter. It will be seen again later how housing has been the area of policy where the Conservative move to the Right has been most marked and has had the most obvious implementation successes. However, the treatment of private tenants supplied Labour with an issue which it was to exploit in the run up to the 1964 general election.

Education - Expansion and Equality

The story of education policy between 1951 and 1964 is an interesting one. Whilst there was no significant legislation, the Conservatives saw themselves as responsible for implementing the war-time Act of 1944, the product of the work of one of their leaders, R.A. Butler. Thus they were concerned to strengthen public sector education, where extensive expenditure was necessary to bring down class sizes and to replace the ageing stock of school buildings. Parents' expectations of the education system grew as the nation prospered. A post-war baby boom and the increasing suburbanisation of British society added to the need for new schools. Hence, Conservative ministers saw themselves as the administrators of an evolving public education system. At least two of these ministers, David Eccles and Sir Edward Boyle, took a distinct pride in this role (see Kogan, 1971, for an interview with Boyle, carried out in 1970 after he had left politics).

The 1944 Act has been seen as a measure which, whilst it set up a secondary education system which was expected to be tri-partite and selective, offered a framework in which a variety of approaches could flourish. The tri-partite idea did not really take off inasmuch as there was a failure to establish an effective system of technical schools. The evidence seems to be that the ministry and the education profession were ambivalent about this development, and no minister really pushed the idea (Sanderson, 1991). A bi-partite system of grammar schools and secondary modern schools, with little public doubt about the preferability of places for children in the former, thus became the dominant model. Yet it would be too simplistic to portray the establishment of this divided system, with children sorted between prestigious and stigmatised systems by means of rigid selection tests, as the hallmark of Conservative education policy at this time. The government was prepared to let local authorities choose their systems, and a minority chose comprehensive education. By 1965 over 8 per cent of children in public education in England and Wales were in comprehensive schools, of which there were 262 (Benn and Simon, 1972, p.102).

But even more significant than this demonstration of acceptance of local choice was the way in which evidence on the drawbacks of a selective system of education was assembled by a series of government sponsored reports. The crucial source here was a statutory advisory committee, whose establishment was required under the 1944 Act, in a section carrying forward an earlier arrangement. That section required that a Central Advisory Council should 'advise the Secretary of State upon such matters connected with education theory and practice as they think fit and upon any questions referred to them by him' (1944 Education Act, section 4 (1)). The prior emphasis on what *they* think fit is interesting. This Council produced a memorable series of reports: on early leaving (Central Advisory Council for Education, 1954), on education between 15 and 18 (ibid., 1959), and on the education of less academic children (ibid, 1963). At the end of the Conservatives' period of office they were also charged to investigate primary education, an influential report on this appeared after Labour had gained power (ibid., 1967). In a manner which today seems strange, and honourable, the Conservative government thus contributed to the growing critique of the selective bi-partite system. Such use of independent advice and research rarely occurs nowadays.

Finally, the contribution of the 1951-64 government to the evolution of education policy included the first steps towards the expansion of higher education. The Prime Minister set up the Robbins Committee to examine higher education in 1961. It reported in 1963 (Cmnd. 2154), its proposal for the growth of the university sector being warmly accepted by the government. The government had earlier taken steps to stimulate the development of technical education at a higher level, an initiative which, it has been suggested (Sanderson, 1991), was subsequently undermined by the absorption of the most successful of these ventures into the university system.

The Conservative record on education was one the party boasted about in 1964 in its election manifesto in the following way:

> Education is the most rapidly developing feature of our social outlay. Its share of the expanded national wealth has risen since 1951 from three per cent to five per cent, and will go on rising.

It went on to pledge to raise the school leaving age to 16 and to expand higher education.

To sum up, whilst the Conservatives were generally attached to the selective principle and certainly did nothing to curb the role of the private sector, education can be seen as an area of policy in which, during the period 1951-64, many new schools were built and public expenditure on

education grew steadily.   Innovation was slow to occur, but the government was able to countenance a situation in which its own Advisory
Council encouraged a debate about the shortcomings of the system,
providing powerful evidence for the advocates of more egalitarian
policies, particularly for the development of comprehensive secondary
education.   The key point to be made about this last phenomenon was that
this was very much an era in which professional rather than political
concerns were allowed to dominate the education agenda.

Pensions - The Emergence of a Need for New Initiatives

Social security was another policy area where the 1951-64 governments
were generally content to leave the system alone.   However, when
inflation occurs income maintenance systems cannot be left entirely
unaltered.   It forces uprating, which pushes up costs and then tempts
governments to make cuts, which have to be effected either by evading
full uprating or changing the system.   The relatively low inflation rates of
this period, by comparison with the years, enabled benefit rate uprating
to be an erratic and less than annual process.   In later years a requirement
for annual reviews was built in, and sophisticated pressure groups
emerged to challenge stratagems used to evade full uprating.   There was
a pension increase in September 1951, just a month before the Conservatives came to power.   The next was just a year later.   There then followed
an almost three-year gap to April 1955 (there was an election next
month!).   The subsequent increases were in January 1958, April 1961 and
May 1963 (to be fair none of these was very close to electioneering
periods).

It is not only changes in the cost of living which push up social security
costs; so too do increases in demand.   For this period one crucial factor
influencing demand was the provision in the initial legislation to allow
new national insurance contributors to qualify for a full pension if they
retired ten years or more after the start of the scheme.   This implied a big
leap in expenditure on national insurance pensions in 1958.   Another
factor was the growth in the numbers of the elderly (a theme running
throughout the period covered by this book).   Other demand factors were
fairly stable at this time, particularly because unemployment remained
low.

Hence the cost of pensions became a live issue.   The government was
in a dilemma about this.   On the one hand it faced a substantial need for
an expenditure increase, to be funded either by increased insurance
contributions or tax.   On the other hand it was criticised for any

reluctance to raise pension rates. This reluctance made it necessary for increasing numbers of pensioners to apply for means-tested social security benefits to supplement their basic pension. The Labour Party attacked them on this issue. The government appointed a committee to examine the financial problems of provision for old age (the Phillips Report, Cmd. 9333, 1954). This expressed doubts about the feasibility of making significant improvements to insurance pensions. It recommended raising the pension age, an interesting reflection of the full employment of this period. It was nevertheless something the government was not prepared to do, though policies were developed to encourage people to go on working beyond pension age.

It was ironic that the cost pressures on the insurance pensions scheme came from the largely better off new pensioners who had not been contributors before 1948, whilst the group forced to apply for means-tested supplements was poorer people who were more likely to have been long-term contributors. Obviously, in the short run, the government could do little about that problem. However, consideration of it did point towards one direction for reform. Pensioners who needed means-tested supplements were typically those without any form of additional private pension. The new group of insurance pensioners, by contrast, often had benefits from private schemes. If earnings-related schemes could be made universal for future pensioners, through the provision of a state-run contributory scheme, then the government could take in more revenue to help to fund its present commitments from increased contributions towards future cover. Such is the typical 'pay as you go' character of state provisions that devices of this kind can be used to solve a political dilemma.

It was Labour which initially made progress towards the planning of earnings-related pensions. A Fabian pamphlet (Abel-Smith and Townsend, 1955) first set out the basis for this kind of contributory scheme. The Labour Party itself developed this into a proposal for 'national superannuation' in 1957. There were some crucial difficulties to be sorted out concerning the nature of the long-run guarantee and the speed at which it would be phased in. There was also an issue to be resolved about the extent to which the scheme would be compulsory, as opposed to one which would apply only to those not in adequate private schemes. It will be seen later that the Labour Party took a long while to decide how to deal with these dilemmas once it returned to power.

However, the Conservatives determined that they should develop an additional contributory scheme, but solely for those not contributing to private pensions. Their approach was modest in scope, but it did play the role outlined above of relieving the funding problems of the 'Beveridge' flat-rate scheme. The new graduated pensions system was enacted in the 1959 National Insurance Act. Its income helped to fund pensions increases in 1961 and 1963. These increases were, however, insufficient to lift many existing pensioners off means-tested supplements. Increases in the rates for the latter continued to keep pace with insurance benefit rate increases. Despite its own record, Labour continued to criticise the Conservatives on this issue. Labour's further difficulties with the same problem on returning to power will be examined in the next chapter.

Health

The first Minister of Health in this period combined the office with leadership of the House of Commons. The office was not in the Cabinet until 1962. It would appear that only two ministers had much impact upon the department; these were the second one, Iain Macleod, who held office from 1952 to 1955, and Enoch Powell, who was minister from 1960 to 1962. Yet even Macleod saw his tenure of the office in terms of ensuring continuity of administration rather than political change. He said he would like to be the first Minister of Health who did not pass any legislation (Fisher, 1973, p.93).

Nevertheless as the steadily rising cost of the service had already caused concern to the Labour government, it was similarly bound to be a concern to the Conservatives. In 1952 the government introduced prescription charges. It also set up a committee to investigate the cost of the National Health Service (the Guillebaud Committee). This body reported in 1956. It concluded that no significant administrative changes were necessary and confined itself to making a variety of detailed observations about ways to increase efficiency. Its crucial observation was as follows:

> The rising cost of the Service in real terms during the years 1948-54 was kept within narrow bounds; while many of the services provided were substantially expanded and improved during the period. Any charge that there has been widespread extravagance... whether in respect of the spending of money or the use of manpower is not borne out by our evidence (Guillebaud Report, 1956, Cmd. 9663, p.269).

Despite this report the Treasury continued to express its concerns about the costs of the NHS and, in a package of cuts brought forward by the Chancellor Peter Thorneycroft in 1957, there were proposals to take the non-hospital ophthalmic service out of the NHS and, more significantly, to impose boarding charges on hospital in-patients (Lowe, 1989).

Thorneycroft's package of cuts, which also included a reduction in the Family Allowance, was rejected by the Cabinet. Thorneycroft resigned with his two junior ministers, Birch and Powell. This incident, dismissed as 'a little local difficulty' by the Prime Minister, has in later years come to be seen both as the high point of consensus Conservatism and alternatively as the first stirring of the harsher type of Conservatism which was to emerge in the 1970s and 1980s (Horne, 1989, vol. 2, pp.75-9).

Boarding charges figured as a suggestion in the *One Nation* pamphlet (Macleod and Maude, 1950); they subsequently emerged from time to time in Right-wing proposals for the NHS but were not introduced. However, hospital stays have become shorter and shorter, and the care of many of the chronically ill has moved out to the community and the local authorities (where means-tested boarding charges are very much part of personal social services policy).

One significant piece of new legislation relating to health services passed in the period of Conservative rule, was the Mental Health Act of 1959, based upon the recommendations of a Royal Commission which reported in 1957 (the Percy Commission). This shifted the treatment of mentally ill people away from the processes of certification based upon the old Lunacy Acts, making treatment and hospitalisation voluntary wherever possible, with compulsory powers reserved for exceptional problems and under firm professional control.

Much other health service policy-making concerned the search for a framework for paying the various groups of doctors in an attempt to satisfy their strongly voiced demands without sacrificing ministerial control.

Rudolph Klein sums up health policy in this era in two pungent observations at the beginning and end of a chapter entitled the 'politics of consolidation'. At the beginning he says:

> In 1958 the House of Commons held a celebratory debate to mark the tenth anniversary of the creation of the National Health Service. It turned out to be an exercise in mutual self-congratulation as Labour and Conservative speakers competed with each other in taking credit for the achievement of the NHS (Klein, 1989, p.31).

At the end, however, he concludes:

> The triumph of the 1950s was to make the NHS work; but the price paid for creating a consensus - for putting the emphasis on achieving financial respectability, administrative stability and professional accountability - was to introduce a bias towards inertia (ibid. p.58).

For Klein the problems of inertia particularly concerned the failure to address the health service's split structure and the acceptance of professional dominance. Both of these issues were to be addressed again and again in the later period with which this book is concerned. For others, the problems that were later to assume most significance were the failure of the system to narrow health inequalities and the overall tendency for the service to be a 'national illness service' rather than one with an overall concern for the determinants of the nation's health. As far as the latter theme is concerned, it is interesting to note that one of the major legislative achievements in this period was the Clean Air Act of 1956, thrust upon the Department of Health by pressure groups and first brought before Parliament in a private members' measure promoted by a Conservative backbencher. This, perhaps classic example of 'pluralism' has, in retrospect, played a key role in improving the nation's health by largely eliminating the traditional 'smog' problem in London and other large cities.

Conclusion: 13 Wasted Years?

The subtitle for this concluding section is taken from a Labour electoral gibe used in 1984. It is today perhaps also a gibe with which many modern Tories on the Right of the party may agree, for different reasons. The object of this book is however not to judge but to explain. What is to be explained is that, despite the fact that critics on the Right were beginning to mount their subsequently influential critique, these Conservative governments saw themselves principally as cautious consolidators of the welfare state.

It was suggested at the beginning of this chapter that leading members of this still very aristocratic Conservative party were principally interested in international and colonial affairs. A rising young Conservative like Iain Macleod recognised that the fact that so few politicians were interested in social policy offered a quick route to ministerial office. Once in office, politicians like Macmillan, Macleod and Eccles saw their roles as champions of their own department, with reputations to make by advancing social policy. A classic pattern was established, subsequently documented by the American political scientists Heclo and Wildavsky (1974), of social spending departments fighting the Treasury, and sometimes indirectly each other, for a share of the growing national cake. Near the end of the era the Plowden Committee (Cmnd. 1432, 1961) identified a need to coordinate this process in order to enhance expenditure control.

Social policy growth was enhanced by two other features of this era. One was a considerable Conservative nervousness about the electoral consequences of being seen as hostile to the interests of pensioners, to the strengthening of the National Health Service or to the prevention of unemployment. Opinion poll data suggested that these were issues that the Labour party could exploit. Butler and Stokes pointed out:

> ... how one-sided the public's support for increased outlays for the social services were in the early 1960s. The spontaneous references... were overwhelmingly angled towards increased government expenditure on pensions and housing. Of those who mentioned social welfare issues, fewer than one in ten touched restrictionist themes (1971, pp.414-15).

The other was the readiness to turn to experts for advice on social policy issues. Thus, in education the Central Advisory Council had a significant impact on the agenda, whilst in health the Guillebaud Committee drew heavily upon the services of two advisers close to the Labour party, Richard Titmuss and Brian Abel-Smith. These features contributed to the view that this was an the era of consensus in social policy, an era when pluralistic policy-making came to be accepted as the dominant feature of the British scene. The Conservatives eyed nervously the potential electoral impact of the slowly developing range of interest groups: pensioners' organisations, patients' organisations, parents dissatisfied with the impact of 11 plus, and so on. It was believed that the Conservatives owed their electoral success to this sensitivity. Hence, in summing up their analysis of the 1959 election, in which Macmillan had won support by stressing the maintenance of growing prosperity, David Butler and Richard Rose noted:

> Labour, moreover, had no monopoly of social reform. The Conservatives could point to their maintenance of the welfare state (Butler and Rose, 1960, p.199).

Later chapters will chart the emergence of a more ideologically oriented Conservative party willing to calculate which interest groups it could disregard.

5   The Labour Governments 1964-70

Introduction

Labour narrowly won the election of 1964 with 44.1 per cent of the vote to the Conservatives' 43.4 per cent. They gained a majority of 13 over the Conservatives (and Ulster Unionists) and an overall majority of only four. For a government committed to new initiatives this narrow majority was a disadvantage. However, the new Prime Minister, Harold Wilson, was determined to make an initial impact, modelled on Kennedy's initial 100 days in the United States in 1960. Success in doing this would then make it possible to call another election to strengthen Labour in the House of Commons. Wilson succeeded in this respect. There was a further election in March 1966 at which Labour won 48.7 per cent of the votes cast. The Conservatives got 41.9 per cent. Labour secured 363 seats, in comparison with 253 for the Conservatives and their allies and 12 for the Liberals. In retrospect Labour's most striking achievements in policy terms belong to the initial period when the party governed with a tiny majority. Key legislation on social security and on private rents was on the statute book before the 1966 election.

The performance of the Labour government of 1964-70 has attracted various inquests (Townsend and Bosanquet, eds., 1972; Beckerman, 1972; Ponting, 1989), with disappointment about its record a dominant theme. While the purpose of this book is not to criticise, it is relevant to note that Labour claimed it would effect substantial changes and to ask why the government fell short of its own aspirations. Most of the contributors to the volume edited by Townsend and Bosanquet were particularly dissatisfied with Labour's achievements. But one contributor, Peter Kaim Caudle, firmly tried to set that disappointment in context:

> A future Labour government will have to start by 'putting the economy right'. A progressive social policy is hardly possible with a huge deficit in the balance of payments or a stagnating economy slipping into unemployment. The reason for this cannot be blamed on the bankers or the Treasury Knights

but is caused by the unwillingness of doctors and dockers, of dustbinmen and teachers, of printers and seamen to pay more taxes, whether directly or indirectly, out of incomes which do not rise sufficiently fast to give them the higher standards of living to which they consider themselves entitled. The 'passion for equality' is a minority creed (Townsend and Bosanquet, eds., 1972, p.160).

Here Peter Kaim Caudle sets out very clearly two linked explanations of the Labour record: (1) economic problems subverted social policy goals, and (2) there was a lack of popular support for radical redistribution in a context of low growth.

Another evaluation of the Labour record by a sympathetic group of economists, whilst critical of the way the economy was managed, concluded that the Labour record on redistribution was quite a good one:

> ... there was an improvement in the distribution of income, both vertical and horizontal... The main reason for this seems to have been increases in cash benefits - National Insurance and Supplementary Benefits, and family allowances. Increases in benefits in kind, taking the form of a rapid rise in the provision of health and educational services, were also an important influence.
>
> To have promoted a measurable improvement in the distribution of income against the background of the deplorably slow rate of growth of output permitted by its macro-economic policies was one of the Labour Government's main achievements... (Stewart in Beckerman, ed., 1972, pp.110-11).

Thus whilst Kaim Caudle suggests there was a situation in which Labour's social policy aspirations had to be seen as secondary to its economy management concerns, Stewart suggests that Labour's achievements were considerable *despite* its failure to manage the economy effectively. Then, as in the late 1940s, it is also important to bear in mind the extent to which the continuation of foreign and defence policies, in which Britain contrived to play a world role, also imposed limits upon the room for manoeuvre at home (Ponting, 1989). This both imposed substantial and competing public expenditure pressures for social policy, and contributed to a situation on which American support was seen as conditional upon 'orthodox' management of the economy. Nevertheless defence expenditure did fall a little in real terms across the period of Labour rule. Public expenditure accounts show it to have been the equivalent of 1,829 million pounds (at 1963 prices) in 1964 and 1,526 million in 1970 (Central Statistical Office, 1972).

Walker's analysis of public expenditure data (also used in the last chapter to analyse the performance of the 1951-64 Conservatives) shows a slightly lower growth rate for GDP, compared to the earlier period, of 2.6 per cent per annum between 1964-70. However, there was a distinct jump in the proportion of that going into public social expenditure, from 19.3 per cent to 23.4 per cent (Walker, ed., 1982, p.28). The annual average growth of public expenditure was 5.9 per cent. The individual sector which increased most was social security at 6.5 per cent. It was followed by health and personal social services expenditure at 6.3 per cent, education at 5.5 per cent and housing at 4.0 per cent (ibid., p.29).

In exploring the politics of the 1964-70 period, there is a need to give some attention to the personality of the Prime Minister and to the way the government as a whole conducted its business. Harold Wilson has been characterised as a civil servant turned politician (Hennessy and Seldon, 1987). Such a judgement has two implications for this discussion. One was that whilst he presented himself and his government as a moderniser of institutions, he approached this task in practice rather slowly and cautiously, with considerable respect for traditional ways of doing business. The clearest example of this is the review of the civil service, where a very thorough investigation led by Lord Fulton (Cmnd. 3638, 1968), ultimately led to very little change. In the field of social policy there was also a very full review of institutions, with a Royal Commission to examine local government and the initiation of a debate on the structure of the health service. But this also proceeded very slowly and cautiously, with a very full consultation of the many interested parties. As a consequence changes were still under consideration when Labour fell from power in 1970.

The other point about Wilson as a typical civil servant involved his continuing concern to ensure that all points of view were taken into account. A less complimentary way of putting this is to suggest that he was in many respects more a political manager than a leader (see the assessment of Wilson in Morgan, 1992, for example). However, that may have been an essential attribute in order to cope with the complexities of Labour politics. From one perspective Wilson can be seen as ever suspicious of conspiracies, ever concerned to balance the interests of his fractious team, and as a consequence failing to provide a clear lead. From another perspective his cautious approach was justified by the threats he faced, and thus essential for the preservation of his position and the protection of the Labour movement he led. The result, however, was a government forever in danger of losing sight of its own goals and aspirations.

Social Security - Back to Beveridge?

The 1964 Labour manifesto had a large section devoted to social security. It started with the following:

> Social security benefits - retirement and widows' pension, sickness and unemployment pay - have been allowed to fall below minimum levels of human need. Consequently one in four of National Insurance pensioners today are depending upon means-tested National Assistance benefits. Labour will reconstruct our social security system.

That pledge sounds like a commitment to a 'back to Beveridge' policy, improving social insurance and diminishing the role of means-tested benefits. The whole section ended, however, with the proviso that 'the key factor in determining the speed at which the new and better levels of benefit can be introduced will be the rate at which the British economy can advance'.

In practice, under the shadow of that condition, what was problematical about Labour's plan was the comprehensive character of its aspirations to reform social security. A central contradiction in the whole scheme was that the Party proposed both to reform National Assistance and to improve National Insurance. The approach proposed for the former, and given top priority, was what was called an 'incomes guarantee' which would provide:

> ... a new national minimum benefit. Those whose incomes fall below the new minimum will receive as of right, and without recourse to National Assistance, an income supplement.

Clearly the objective was to lift many existing beneficiaries off assistance whilst improving insurance so that future claimants of the latter benefits would not need supplementation. But as the government was soon to learn when uprating the existing benefits, there is a difficult interaction between the systems. Increases of insurance benefit rates faster than assistance rates led to the criticism that gains in the former were simply offset by losses of the latter. Moving the two together simply maintained the status quo. The use of scarce resources which provided the most obvious gain for the poorest was to raise assistance faster than insurance rates. However, that let the goal of reducing dependence upon means tests fade further into the distance!

In addition there were issues to be addressed about the relationship between benefits for people out of work and the wages (or benefits) secured by those in work. This was a matter which increasingly troubled the 1964-70 government. Yet it was disregarded by the 1964 manifesto: a statutory minimum wage was not on the agenda, nor was any proposal to raise Family Allowance. Moreover the devices actually resorted to in efforts to deal with this issue (devising or encouraging new means-tested benefits to assist with rates and rents) were not considered at this time.

This section will look, first, at the policies developed to enhance National Insurance. It will then turn to the reform of Assistance. Then, it will end with the issues about the development of policies to help the working poor.

As far as National Insurance was concerned, there was a contrast between the comparatively speedy action on benefits other than pensions, and the difficulties the government experienced with its 'national superannuation scheme'. Most of the manifesto pledges on the other benefits were fulfilled by 1966. The widows' earning rule was abolished, and earnings-related supplements were introduced into the sickness and unemployment benefit schemes. The general pledge to link the uprating of National Insurance benefits in line with earnings was not literally fulfilled, but there were upratings in 1964, 1967 and 1969. A pledge to introduce a redundancy pay scheme (not an insurance benefit, but nevertheless relevant to this section) was fulfilled. All these measures were enacted without much difficulty. They were not particularly costly; indeed, earnings-related benefits were funded from increased contributions - a change with implications for the earnings/benefits relationship to be considered later. The benefits from these changes were most apparent for workers experiencing short-term problems of loss of work through sickness and unemployment, largely members of Labour's main funders, at that time, the industrial trade unions.

Although Labour had first committed itself to national superannuation in 1957, the government did not produce a White Paper proposing legislation until 1969, the year before it fell from power. This delay seems to have been the result of a combination of factors. First, the politician particularly linked with the preparatory work on the scheme in opposition, Richard Crossman, was appointed to other posts and did not end up with responsibility for social security until 1968. His predecessors, according to his account (Crossman, 1976, p.429), seemed to have accepted a civil service view of the need to proceed slowly. A civil servant's account of this, however, blames Labour's other social security preoccupations (Ellis, 1989, p.23). The latter also suggests that: 'The economic problems which preceded the 1967 devaluation also made an earlier increase in pensions expenditure seem unattractive' (ibid.). This comment can only be understood if it is recognised that, whilst the promise of national superannuation lay in the future, the government faced a political dilemma because it wanted to do as much as possible for existing pensioners. It would be open to damaging criticism, from its own supporters as much as anyone, if it produced a scheme which advantaged a generation whose retirement lay 20 years or more ahead and provided nothing extra for current pensioners. Yet big increases in contributions would be problematical at a time when the government was striving to hold back pay rises.

There is a most interesting piece in the Crossman diaries on this theme. First, he reports 'defeating' a delegation from the Trades Union Congress in an argument in which the latter asserted that the proposed scheme's disregard of current pensioners was a 'fatal defect' whereas he insisted that this was unavoidable (Crossman, vol.3, 1977, p.176). Then he goes on to the following reflection:

> In the course of all these consultations I have found... that my own personal position has been fatally undermined. I am fighting both the Ministry and the Treasury in support of a properly funded scheme. Alas, the unanswerable Treasury argument is that if we piled up millions in the fund it would only be appropriated for the existing pensioners. We must therefore really accept pay-as-you-go.

Interestingly Janet Morgan, the editor of the diaries, (they were published posthumously) comments in a footnote that 'in real terms any pension scheme is "pay as you go"'. This is a reference to the way in which government accounting practices treat contributions as income for use at the time received. Crossman, who prided himself on his ability to manage civil servants, was perhaps a little out of his depth here; his editor suggests that he did not really understand Treasury practice. However, it would have been possible to treat pension contributions differently. Governments rarely 'fund' state pensions, but there is an example of this practice in Singapore where the consequence has been the ownership of assets by the state-sponsored pension fund.

Legislation to enact the national superannuation scheme was introduced in December 1969. It included provisions for individuals to 'opt out' if they were contributing to approved private pension schemes. They would pay lower contributions. However, the Prime Minister decided to call a general election before the Bill could complete all its Parliamentary stages. Hence, the measure was lost, for the time being (it was to reappear and be enacted, slightly modified - despite an intervening effort to deal with the same issue by the Conservatives - under the Labour government elected in 1974).

In its efforts to replace National Assistance by the 'income guarantee' proposal, the Government fell far short of its original objective. It did abolish National Assistance in 1966. But it replaced it with something remarkably similar, tempting the cynic to suggest that it was trying to create the impression that it had fulfilled its promise by a change of name. The new scheme, Supplementary Benefit, was an improvement on its predecessor inasmuch as certain discretionary powers were curbed. In particular it was now impossible to reduce benefits to pensioners below a statutorily guaranteed minimum (something which had in practice rarely occurred before the change). The administration of the scheme was partially integrated into the rest of the social security system. The aim was to simplify administration and reduce stigma by making rights more certain and by reducing the range of discretionary variations. In practice some of the attempted simplification did not work, notably the introduction of a 'long-term' rate of benefit designed to replace some discretionary extras (see Hill, 1974; Prosser, 1981).

The change had very little impact upon the problem of stigma, and its equivocal granting of rights increased disputes over decision-making about claims. It is difficult to say whether the increased level of controversy over means testing was a product of this half-baked reform or due to extraneous developments. During the 1960s new political movements were developing, and ideas about 'welfare rights' campaigns were crossing the Atlantic (Titmuss, 1971; Bull, 1980). An effective new pressure group for poor families (the Child Poverty Action Group) was set up. The net political effect was that during this period means testing was lifted from relative obscurity to become, and remain, at the centre of political controversy - both with a big 'P' at the national level and with a small one at the 'street-level' where benefit decisions were being made.

In an essay in Hall, Land, Parker and Webb (1978), the last named examines the failure of the income guarantee proposal. He explores the extent to which this might have been attributable to economic concerns, discussed elsewhere in this chapter, or to the desire to get something onto the statute book ready for the 1966 election. These were obviously factors, but in combination with them, Webb suggests, attention needs to be directed to problems related to political feasibility. The government wanted the scheme to be operated by the Inland Revenue; that department was resistant and would have had to make changes to a range of related processes dealing with taxation (this problem cropped up again with some of the ideas of the 1970-74 Conservative government). There was also a need to resolve a range of issues about disincentive effects, about variable incomes and about varying needs (particularly rents). These, too, undermined later approaches to means-test reform.

But overall, was there not a conflict here inasmuch as a government with an overall commitment to the Beveridge principle of putting insurance at the centre of the social security system and means tests in a residual 'safety net' role, was here flirting with a very different and perhaps incompatible approach involving a kind of 'negative income tax'? That same conflict was central to the third area of policy to be discussed in this section, measures for the earning poor.

Webb's discussion of the last years of National Assistance shows how Parliamentary criticism of that scheme focused upon the 'wage stop' amongst the issues which were debated (ibid., 454-5). The wage stop was a rule designed to prevent unemployed and temporarily sick claimants of National Assistance ·from securing more in benefit than they could earn when in work. Some Labour members wanted this rule to be abolished, but the minister resisted this. She argued that '"the crux of the problem was family allowances" and that "scandalously low wages" were a matter for the TUC' (Hall, Land, Parker and Webb, ibid., quoting Margaret Herbison, p.455).

At about the same tim·: evidence was being brought to light concerning the numbers of families with breadwinners in full-time work whose incomes were below National Assistance levels (Abel-Smith and Townsend, 1965). Interestingly the Conservative opposition, whose social security spokesperson at this time was Margaret Thatcher, seemed to agree that there was a dilemma about the wage stop rather than suggest that benefits were too high (HC Deb vol. 704, cols 331-2, 336 and 340-2).

In 1965 a group of concerned people submitted a memorandum to the government on poverty. This memorandum drew in particular upon an article by Tony Lynes, which set out the need for a family policy which addressed the issues about low income, taxation and Family Allowances. Lynes temporarily became a civil servant in Margaret Herbison's department, but was consigned to a relatively junior position in the hierarchy at the insistence of the civil service. He resigned, disillusioned, in 1966 to become the first full-time official of the organisation set up by the original authors of the memorandum, the Child Poverty Action Group (this account draws upon fuller discussions of these events in Banting, 1979, and McCarthy, 1986).

The Child Poverty Action Group became, in due course, both an effective advocate of the case for much higher levels of Family Allowance and an overall critic of government policies towards the poor. It also gradually took upon itself a role at the centre of the growing welfare rights movement: providing direct advice, fighting tribunal and court cases, training advocates and disseminating information on the detailed rules relating to means tests (see McCarthy, 1986). Its pressure group activities will receive attention from time to time throughout the rest of this book.

The government's first response to the demand for increased Family Allowance was in most respects merely a symbolic one. The allowance for the fourth, and subsequent, children in families was increased by five shillings (25p) in October 1967. The campaign for something better than this continued. It was argued that one way to help to fund an increase in Family Allowance was to eliminate the income tax-based child allowance which delivered more help to the better off than to the poorer families. This argument was described as calling for the 'claw-back' of the tax allowance in order to increase Family Allowance. · Banting has shown how the arguments about 'clawback' split the Government. James Callaghan, who was Chancellor until 1967, advanced the orthodox view of the Treasury and Inland Revenue that issues about tax and benefits should not be mixed. He believed that an attack on tax allowances would be unpopular with many working-class earning men. He preferred the idea of a means-tested family benefit. Clearly, within the civil service work was proceeding to develop such a proposal, which surfaced with the next government. Callaghan failed to enlist trade union support for his view. In the past trade unions had been suspicious of Family Allowance seeing it as a device to lower wages (see Land, in Hall, Land, Parker and Webb, 1978). By this time, however, they had become strong supporters and accepted the 'clawback' concept.

After Callaghan left the Treasury, his successor, Roy Jenkins, moved very cautiously forward on clawback. There were Family Allowance increases for all eligible children (bear in mind that first children did not qualify at this time) in 1968 in two stages, adding up to ten shillings (50p) in all, offset against reductions in tax allowances. This was a modest measure which did not eliminate tax allowances.

The government continued to be wary of extending the measure. That caution was inevitably influenced by the extent to which inflation had lowered the tax threshold so that many relatively low-income families were becoming beneficiaries of tax allowances. The Child Poverty Action Group, the Directorship of which passed from Tony Lynes to Frank Field in 1969, lobbied very hard for further concessions on Family Allowance in Jenkins' last budget. They did not get them. Hence, in Banting's words:

> ... as the 1970 election approached and no further action was taken, the group took off their gloves. They attacked the Government's social policy record

and argued that the poor had actually become poorer under Labour. The conclusion of this phase of British social policy was a bitter public exchange between CPAG and the Labour Government during the run up to the election campaign (Banting, 1979, p.108).

In the next chapter the examination of the subsequent stages in the argument between advocates of increased Family Allowance and advocates of a means-tested system will explore further the dilemma of a social policy pressure group, whose natural allies were in the Labour government, in this kind of situation.

But before leaving the discussion of Labour's social security policy, it is necessary to note how there was yet another area where the government's ambivalence about means tests had important consequences. That area was policy on rates and rents. The problems about local authority property taxation as an inflexible and comparatively regressive form of taxation (relative at least to income tax, as will be seen in chapter 8 that was a much more regressive alternative was to come along later) were on the political agenda from the 1960s onward, as government policies on education and the personal social services pushed up local government expenditure.   In 1966 the Labour government enacted a measure providing a system of means-tested rate rebates for low-income households.

This could be treated as an isolated and ad hoc example of the extension of means testing by a government with a general commitment against this device were it not for a series of efforts to encourage local authorities to consider developing means-tested rent rebates for their council tenants. A housing White Paper in 1965 warned that subsidy increases would be slight and urged local authorities to use rebates to concentrate their benefits on low-income tenants. In 1967 a Ministry of Housing circular reinforced this view and provided recommendations on various forms means tests should take.   Then in 1968 a Prices and Incomes Board Report commended rebates as an alternative to general rent increases. It argued that the government should develop a national scheme.   This recommendation was disregarded, but once again the scene was set for the next Conservative government.   In other words the provision of rate rebates at this time and the encouragement of rent rebates may be seen as the beginning of a process of policy change which was eventually to lead to a universal system of means-tested housing benefits. The solution of Beveridge's 'problem of rent' for the social security system perhaps lay this way.   But it may also be seen as the period when public housing policy began to move towards what has been described as residualisation (Malpass, 1990), when council housing became increasingly housing for the poor, supported through targeted (means-tested) subsidies, rather than through general support to this sector.

This third and final part of this section needs a brief summing up. What is being suggested is that the government was (as the contrast between the first two sections of this discussion suggests) on the horns of a dilemma, wanting both to extend National Insurance and to use means tests to attack that poverty to which a cautious balanced-budget approach to social insurance made it difficult to respond. In the issues concerning families supported by low earner breadwinners and concerning the rents and rates of those outside the supplementary benefit scheme the government found further reasons for flirting with extensions of means testing. It resisted them in the former case but not in the latter. Meanwhile the 'permanent government' - the civil service - was clearly less inhibited in advancing its thinking about means tests.

Housing

The discussion of rent rebates near the end of the last section provides a natural link to this section. It will be seen again in later chapters that the fact that rebates are both aspects of social security and ingredients of housing policy leads to difficulties about the relationship between these two, until the 1960s, rather separate policy sectors. By the time the Conservatives fell from power in 1964, a considerable amount of work had been done on policies designed to target subsidies of public sector housing towards lower income people. Labour resisted taking on that agenda. Yet when it increased subsidies to new public housing, it altered the basis of central government aid from the old simple system of an amount per house for a specific period to one which was the equivalent of a reduction of the rate at which lower authorities borrowed money. This measure had the effect, at the time, of giving strong support to new investment. In the longer run it added to the complexity of the subsidy system, since local authority receipts from central government were made up of a complicated mix of subsidies based upon various schemes stretching back 40 years. Whilst, as has been seen, the government advocated (but did not enforce rebates) in the context of an unreformed subsidy system, as Malpass points out:

> ... a growing number of writers, politicians, academics and housing practitioners framed their demands for rent rebates within an entirely new approach to housing finance, in which rebates were linked to fair rents and deficit subsidies (Malpass, 1990, p.107).

Earlier in the same book, Malpass characterises Labour's approach to council housing at this time in the following way:

> The Labour governments of the 1960s had none of the confidence in, and commitment to, council housing that had been a feature of the early post-war years. The 1965 White Paper proposed only that the public sector would provide up to half of the annual output of 500,000 dwellings per year that was the target by 1970. The increase in local authority building was excused in terms of the severity of the contemporary housing problem, rather than being advocated as a desirable development in itself. In this respect Labour's policy was similar to that of the Conservatives in the early 1950s (ibid., p.51).

Without a strong commitment to council housing, the rest of Labour's policies were similarly minor variations from the consensus. The boom in the development in owner-occupied housing continued and, as interest rates rose, the value of the income tax concession on mortgage interest increased. Rather than seeing this as raising problems of equity for public finance, the government's response was to seek ways to extend this benefit to those whose tax payments were too low to benefit from the subsidy. In 1967 an 'option mortgage' scheme was developed to enable this last group to borrow money at a lower rate of interest instead of obtaining what, for them, was a comparatively valueless tax concession. Few took this up; as pointed out elsewhere, the fall in the tax threshold was steadily bringing most low-paid workers into the tax net. No attempt was made to attack this issue in a more systematic way.

In the 1964 election Labour was very ready to try to make political capital from some of the problems arising over private rent control. In the election manifesto the Party pledged itself to:

> Repeal the notorious Rent Act, end further decontrol and restore security of tenure in already decontrolled rented flats and houses. We shall provide machinery for setting rents on a fair basis.

Bold sounding words, but it all depended on what was to be meant by 'fair' rents. What this involved, in the 1965 Rent Act, was the adoption of a procedure under which a system of 'rent officers' was set up to determine rent levels using a curious formula: these officials were required to imagine what rents would be in a market in which there was no scarcity. Such an approach is in itself virtually meaningless. In reality they developed a method of rent determination by means of making comparisons. The concept of fair rent took no account of what the tenant could afford to pay, or - for that matter - how much the landlord could afford to subsidise the tenant. It was left to the 1970-74 Conservative government to introduce a system of rent allowances which might bridge that gap. Crouch and Wolf noted: 'Somewhat surprisingly, perhaps, the overall effect of the Act has been to increase the level of rents' (in Townsend and Bosanquet, 1972, p.42). But was it surprising? This was surely a classic example of a policy which depended crucially upon its implementation process. The recruitment of rent officers, drawn largely from people experienced in the valuation and management of property, with an appeal process to tribunals where similar expertise and interests were represented, made it inevitable that the balance between landlords and tenants was drawn rather closer to the interests of the former than the latter. There are a number of interesting observations on this subject by the minister responsible for this legislation, Richard Crossman. In his diaries he summed up his retrospective assessment of this as one of his failures:

> The first failure undoubtedly relates to rent assessment committees. I didn't succeed in controlling the appointments (Crossman, 1975, p.89).

However, striking a balance between the interests of landlords and tenants is ultimately impossible if rent levels sufficient to give landlords returns comparable to those available from reasonable alternative uses of their asset mean rents beyond the capacity of tenants to pay (in a society where owner-occupation offers a better deal for most people of average income). In the absence of such a balance, many landlords were bound to seek ways to get rid of tenants illegally so that they could sell or set up alternative arrangements that would evade the rent restriction procedures. The legislation excluded furnished dwellings, provoking an inevitable switch into this form of letting. Crossman ruefully reflected on this in a footnote:

> The exclusion of furnished dwellings from the Bill proved to be its fatal flaw... It was urged on me by the officials for purely administrative reasons. They said they couldn't get the Bill done in time. I should have been tough and insisted on including them on Milner Holland's perfectly correct advice. However, this was the recommendation of the Francis Committee in 1971, and the new Conservative Administration promised to implement it (ibid. p.89).

A perfect comment on the consensual civil service domination in so many areas of policy in this period! The Milner Holland Committee was an investigatory committee set up by the Conservatives to look at private renting in London in the light of the scandals that had come to attention after the 1957 Rent Act.

The same consensual tone characterises much of the rest of housing policy in this period. In the last chapter some comments were made on high- rise building and on clearance policies in urban areas. The later years of the 1964-70 government did see a shift away from these policies and, in particular, a developing interest in ways of stimulating housing renewal without rebuilding. These policies continued into the next period of Conservative rule.

Education

The story of education policy over the 1964-70 period is not unlike that of housing policy. Labour from time to time sounded sharply different from its predecessors. The government's performance was not so markedly different. It carried forward its predecessor's commitments to improving the public sector and to expanding higher education.

In the latter sector there was one distinctive innovation - the Open University set up for mature students to obtain higher education. This seems to have been fought through, despite considerable opposition from the Treasury and from the educational establishment, as a special commitment of Harold Wilson to Aneurin Bevan's widow, Jenny Lee (Hall, Land, Parker and Webb, 1975). As far as the rest of higher education was concerned, Labour allowed the group of Colleges of Advanced Technology to become universities, but declared that the next wave of institutions aspiring to that status should remain under local authority control and be designated 'polytechnics'. The Secretary of State asserted that there should be a binary system in which institutions were separate but equal, so that technological education would be fully supported. Nevertheless there continued to be an incremental drift - determined by choices made within higher education and (as in the schools) by the fact that parity of esteem was not a reality - towards the traditional university model of education in arts, pure sciences and social sciences (Sanderson, 1991). At the time of writing this book the polytechnics have just become universities: is this the culmination of this trend or does it imply (as certainly seems to be in the minds of some politicians) that competition from the former polytechnics will now transform the earlier universities.

As far as schools were concerned, Labour seemed to be strongly committed to increased equality. This had led elements within the party to demand action against the privileges of the privately controlled 'public schools'. The government responded to this by setting up the Public Schools Commission, in the words of the 1964 manifesto, to 'advise on the best way of integrating the public schools into the state system of education'. This body laboured long but secured little positive government action. The only significant outcome was a measure forcing the hybrid 'direct grant schools' to choose either full private state or full state-controlled status. This was surely a curiously contradictory achievement for a body supposed to be 'integrating' the private sector into the public one!

However, the central educational issue at this time was the movement towards comprehensive secondary education. On this issue the 1964 election manifesto made a statement which was very revealing of the Labour leadership's ambivalence on an issue on which the party rank and file wanted it to move fast:

> Labour will get rid of the segregation of children into separate schools caused by 11 plus selection: secondary education will be reorganised on comprehensive lines. Within the new system, grammar school education will be extended: in future no child will be denied the opportunity of benefiting from it through arbitrary selection at the age of eleven.

Whilst perhaps one should not carry textual analysis of election manifestos too far, that surely is a rather extraordinary statement. It seems to be saying 'we will go comprehensive but not destroy the grammar schools'. On the one hand then, it was obviously the product of a compromise which therefore predicted slow incremental change. On the other hand it seems to say that the grammar school model would be embodied in the comprehensive system, something which certainly came to pass, with the consequence that insufficient attention was given to the needs of children who found difficulty in achieving significant academic results. The old selective system was largely reproduced inside the new comprehensives (see Ford, 1969).

Labour education policy was led by four Secretaries of State over the party's six years of office, only one of whom, Anthony Crosland (January 1965 to August 1967), took a decisive step towards the extension of comprehensive education. His key action was a circular (10/1965) which requested local education authorities to submit plans for the reorganisation of secondary education along comprehensive lines. It set out various models which might be considered, grasping the nettle that since wholesale building was not possible authorities were likely to need to consider various ways, in addition to the conventional division at the age of 11, to split up their school population in order to enable small buildings to become comprehensive schools for only part of the relevant secondary age group.

This 'government by circular' has provoked subsequent legal analysis focusing upon its legitimacy. Department of Education and Science efforts to force recalcitrant local authorities to change their systems, led to legal battles (see Buxton, 1970). By the end of the period of Labour rule it was apparent that legislation would be necessary to achieve the objective of making the secondary education system totally comprehensive. Nevertheless, change was accelerated over this period. Between 1965 and 1970 the number of comprehensive schools in England and Wales grew from 262 to 1145, and the proportion of the secondary population in these schools grew from 8.5 to 31 per cent. Interestingly, despite the fact that the incoming Conservative minister, Margaret Thatcher, withdrew circular 10/65, the momentum of change continued into the 1970s.

Finally this account of the politics of education under Labour needs to note that the 1964 manifesto pledged the government to raise the school leaving age to 16 at some indeterminant date, by contrast with a Conservative pledge which named the year (1967). Once in government in 1964, a plan to raise the leaving age in 1970 was announced. In January 1968, as part of the package of cuts following devaluation, the implementation date was put back to 1973. This was designed to reduce the need for investment in the period running up to the change. It provoked the resignation of one junior minister.

Institutional Reform in Health and Social Services

The main thrust of the section in the 1964 Labour manifesto on health was to argue that the service had been under-funded. The record of the 1964-70 government shows a significant upward shift in spending (note the figures cited at the beginning of the chapter showing an average annual increase in expenditure of 6.2 per cent per annum by comparison with an increase of 3.1 per cent per annum over the preceding 13 Conservative years).

But the politics of health expenditure is more complicated than a simple concern with overall levels of expenditure. Since the 1970s crude expenditure data have been seen as something for politicians to alternatively boast about and worry about. The issues lying behind it are the powerful factors pushing needs and costs upward, making it necessary to be concerned with efficient outputs. This then feeds back into a political concern about the best way to organise the service. Such a concern began to emerge in the 1960s; its progress onto the political agenda was surely accelerated by strenuous conflict over doctors' remuneration.

Whilst issues about the structure of the NHS had begun to be debated in the 1950s, particularly in the Guillebaud Report (1956), this subject found few echoes in Labour's manifesto. There was an emphasis on the need for a more ambitious 'hospital plan' involving the setting up of more general hospitals. There was also a reference to the need to improve general practitioner services, though interestingly no mention of the development of 'health centres' - an idea popular in Labour party circles at that time. In practice the ministry did seek to encourage the development of health centres by circular, by financial assistance and by stressing the case for group work in its negotiations with general practitioners over salaries and conditions of service. In the manifesto there was also a strong reference to the need to improve the community care services run by the local authorities - 'the most neglected of all the Health Services in recent years'. This issue was not unrelated to the health centres issue since the latter concept generally embodied the idea of the centres as bases for local authority community health services to be operated in close partnership with general practitioners.

Soon after Labour came to power there began what Klein has called the search for 'an organisational fix' (Klein, 1989, p.90). What this particularly involved at this time was a quest, supported by both major political parties, for ways of making the service more unified. The origins of this quest seem to have come rather more from professionals within the service than from politicians. An important influence here was a report of a working party from the British Medical Association and the medical Royal Colleges (Porritt Report, 1962). In 1968 the Government made some proposals for change in a Green Paper (Ministry of Health, 1968). Green Papers were a new idea devised at that time to float ideas for policy change without indicating the determination to act characteristic of a White Paper. The consultative nature of this one was emphasized in its foreword. This made reference to the need to link any changes in the health service with changes to be considered for the structure of local government - on which a Royal Commission was deliberating (Redcliffe Maud, Cmnd. 4040, 1969) -, the structure of the personal social services - on which the Seebohm Committee had just reported (Cmnd. 3703, 1968) - and the future of medical education -the concern of another current report (Todd Commission, Cmnd. 3569, 1968).

The 1968 Green Paper proposed a very simple structure for the health service, merely a system of area boards in England and Wales (it did not address issues concerning Scotland) of about 40 in number, to be as coterminous as possible with local authorities and to be responsible for what were then the three separate parts of the service - hospitals, general practice and the local authority-run community services.

A second Green Paper was produced in 1970 (Department of Health and Social Security, 1970). Its main difference from the first one was prompted by the fact that the Royal Commission on local government had proposed a system involving smaller local government units than anticipated by the 1968 paper. The principle of co-terminosity therefore made necessary rather more area health authorities. 90 were proposed. That change reinforced the view that a regional tier was still needed for the system. About 14 regional health authorities were thus proposed for planning purposes and to carry out certain specialised functions.

The Royal Commission on Local Government revived the debate about the health service which Herbert Morrison had lost in the 1940s. It proposed that health should come under local government control. The second Green Paper rejected this proposal, setting out two reasons. The second of these made little sense at a time when the whole system of local government was under review. It was argued that 'the independent financial resources available to local government are not sufficient to enable them to take over responsibility for the whole health service' (p.7). It was thus surely the first reason that was crucial: 'the professions believe that only a service administered by special bodies on which the professions are represented can provide a proper assurance of clinical freedom' (ibid.). What was proposed instead was a compromise in which both the professions and local government were each to be given a third of the places on the governing bodies, with the other third being appointed by the Secretary of State.

The Labour Government fell before it could proceed to enact its proposals, though its successors continued to work on this structural reform. The next chapter, therefore, returns to this subject.

The reform of the structure of local government was also not carried out within the lifetime of the Labour government. Meanwhile, curiously, the personal social services reorganisation legislation was enacted. This was thus inevitably rather out of line both with reform of the local government system, within which it was embedded, and with reform of the health service, to which it has to relate closely. The former disjunction was particularly significant in getting the new social services departments off to a bad start, because in many areas outside London they had only just been established when local government restructuring required drastic changes. The issue about the relationship between this change and the health service change is more complex. Certainly the social services reform took some tasks away from local authority health departments just before their absorption into area health authorities. However, what now seems more important, viewing this reform retrospectively, is that decisions were taken very quickly in 1969 and 1970 about the split between the two services, especially in areas like the community care of mentally ill or handicapped people which subsequently had to be revised. As a consequence overall boundary problems between the two services continued to give rise to difficulties for a long while.

What is interesting about the reform of the personal social services is that a range of activities in which the party politicians were not particularly interested (which might have been totally absorbed into the health service or might have remained in a fragmented form) were given a separate identity and distinct organisational form as a result of determined lobbying by a small group of social workers and academics. This story has been carefully studied by Phoebe Hall (1976). She shows how a small group, with some links with the Labour leaders, reacted against an initial set of ideas for a family service and exploited the concern for new community initiatives to deal with delinquency (see the report of the Ingleby Committee, 1960) to secure the setting up of the Seebohm Committee in 1965 'to review the organisation and responsibilities of the local authority personal social services in England and Wales and to consider what changes are desirable to secure an effective family service' (Seebohm Report, Cmnd. 3703, 1968, p.11).

The Seebohm Committee recommended the setting up of unified local authority social services departments, bringing together the former children and welfare departments. It considered that the existing local authority health services for mentally ill and handicapped people should come into these new departments, as should educational welfare services. The report had an unfavourable reception. Hall, relying on evidence from the Crossman diaries, reports that the initial reception by the Cabinet was hostile. However, it did not reject the report out of hand but rather referred it to a subcommittee. The medical pressure groups were also hostile to the report. The reaction of the local authority associations was ambivalent, they were 'reluctant to react... before the publication of the Royal Commission on Local Government' (Hall, 1976, p.87).

Yet the Seebohm proposals were enacted almost in their entirety (except for some blurring of the takeover of services from education) in 1970. Why did this happen? In essence Hall's conclusion is that the case for the Seebohm report was advocated effectively by a small group of social work activists operating as 'a coherent political force for the first time' (ibid., p.108). By contrast the medical profession was very preoccupied with the health service changes, the main medical group threatened - the local authority Medical Officers of Health - being particularly affected by those. Hall suggests that the responsible minister was similarly preoccupied by the health reforms and really rather indifferent to issues about the personal social services.

In 1968 the Prime Minister decided to set up an integrated Department of Health and Social Security under a senior minister, Richard Crossman. He initially coordinated the two ministries and then brought them together. Whilst Crossman was one of the most active of the Labour ministers, this meant he had many preoccupations, including social security issues like national superannuation (discussed above) alongside the health service reforms. It is not surprising that he saw the Seebohm reforms as of fairly minor importance. Furthermore, within the NHS itself Crossman had taken a special interest in the evidence from the Ely Inquiry (1969) revealing serious problems in a hospital for mentally handicapped people in Wales. He resolved that the report should be published in full, set up the Hospital Advisory Service as a kind of inspectorate to try to keep an eye on hospitals like this and attempted to give impetus to efforts to reduce the extent of institutionalisation of care of mentally ill and mentally handicapped people. This helped place this neglected issue upon the political agenda. In practice however, policy implementation in this field, which depended upon a very full commitment to change throughout the system, proceeded very slowly. There were to be a succession of further scandals pushing the issue back onto the agenda for Crossman's successors, both Conservative and Labour.

Finally discussion of the record of the 1964-70 Labour government in the health field must include some mention of the issue of prescription charges. The 1964 election manifesto said:

> The most serious attack on the Health Service made by Conservative Ministers has been the increasing burden of prescription charges imposed by them on those least able to pay. These charges will be abolished.

They were abolished in February 1965, only to be reintroduced in 1968. Other charges, for dental and ophthalmic treatment, were not even temporarily suspended. This reversal of policy was slightly tempered by the adoption of exemptions for the chronically sick, the elderly etc. which were more far-reaching than those operating before.

The reversal of what seemed to have been one of Labour's most cherished policies (note that the Prime Minister's main claim to be regarded as radical rested upon the fact that he had resigned with Aneurin Bevan over the original imposition of health service charges) came in a package of expenditure cuts to accompany devaluation in late 1967. Wilson's own account of this decision is disarmingly matter of fact, embedded in discussion of the range of cuts, only one of which - the abandonment of a commitment to raise the school leaving age - provoked a resignation from the government. Clearly he saw the package as a balanced one, anticipating trouble over defence cuts and social policy cuts alike (Wilson, 1974, pp.608-16). Crossman, though not yet the minister responsible that time, confirms this, writing that the Prime Minister and Chancellor 'based their whole package on a fair balance between defence cuts abroad and the slaughter of sacred cows at home' (Crossman, vol. 2, 1976, p.643). It does not require much imagination to guess what bodies of opinion, at home and abroad, this was designed to impress.

The Community Development Project and the Inner Cities

The last of the social policy developments from the period 1964-70 to be discussed involved a small cluster of policies which may be seen, in a sense, as a single initiative. The government developed an approach to social policy in deprived urban areas which was ambiguous in character and inconclusive in outcome, but nevertheless interesting both in terms of the political processes which engendered it and those which it generated itself.

In May 1968 the Prime Minister announced that the government was going to set up 'an urban programme' designed to make money available to supplement other policies in 'relatively small pockets of severe social deprivation' in the cities and towns of Britain. A second set of ideas embraced within this arose from suggestions made by the Plowden Committee on 'Children and their Primary Schools' (Central Advisory Council for Education, 1967) for the concentration of extra educational resources upon 'educational priority areas', where forms of compensatory education could be offered, and for additional provisions for nursery education.

The third element in the urban programme package emerged from the Home Office the next year. This was the setting up of the Community Development Project. This entailed the establishment of action teams in 12 different urban areas to involve citizens in activities designed to tackle problems through subsidised self-help.

Why did these initiatives occur? Most accounts of the original Prime Ministerial intervention cite the growing concern about deteriorating race relations as a crucial 'trigger' factor. Labour's record on race relations was not a happy one. On coming to power it rapidly moved from being a critic of the Conservatives' first step to curb immigration from the Commonwealth in 1962 to tightening restrictions itself in 1965. It attempted to sugar this bitter pill for many of its own supporters by passing anti-discrimination legislation. This was, however, a very weak and largely symbolic measure which ignored the crucial issues of discrimination in housing and the labour market (see Rose, 1969, for further discussion of the politics of race relations at this time).

In 1968 the government decided to deal with the threat to its control policies from increased migration of Asian holders of British passports from East Africa by a further measure which denied even this group a right of entry. It again balanced this with anti-discrimination legislation, of a rather more effective kind this time.

In 1968 the Labour Government clearly felt very threatened by the growing political exploitation of racialism, led by a Conservative MP and former minister, Enoch Powell. It needed, therefore, to try simultaneously to reassure both disadvantaged white inner-city residents who blamed black people for their troubles and also the new immigrants in those same areas for whom it had done little. In addition it did not want its response to be seen as a concern for deprived multi-racial areas at the expense of longstanding areas of deprivation largely unaffected by immigration. An urban policy, which could be described both as a response to racial strife and as 'colour-blind' in its concern about urban deprivation, seemed to fit the bill. Wilson's announcement in May 1968 followed closely upon a notorious speech by Powell in April.

The notion of concentrating resources upon small areas was influenced by American initiatives. In the American case an important driving force was a federal government desire to inject resources which could not be diverted by lower tiers of government (Higgins, 1978). That concern was not particularly evident in these early British initiatives. On the contrary, local authorities were very much partners in the enterprise, expected to put up ideas for funding and often to provide additional resources as well. Later, and particularly in the 1980s, targeted local initiatives rooted in distrust of local government were more in evidence.

The CDP initiatives were ambiguous. They bore a strong mark of American influence carried to Britain by a Home Office civil servant, Derek Morrell. He had a passionate vision of the need for community participation in social policy (Higgins, 1978; Higgins et al., 1983). In Morrell's vision self-help was central; by contrast, the CDP teams came to be dominated by activists with a very different view. They saw the people with whom they worked as trapped by national and local policies they could do little to influence (CDP, 1977). For them community action needed to be not so much self-help as political mobilisation. In this sense, therefore, CDP came to be seen as a threat to local government. It sought, of course, to influence government at all levels, but local government was most immediately in the firing line.

Hence, when the initial CDP projects ended in the early 1970s, the next set of initiatives (Comprehensive Community Programmes) were designed so that local government could play a clearer participating role.

To sum up, the urban programme may be seen as a set of ideas, influenced by American initiatives, carried forward by civil servants and seeming to present politicians with a way of responding to racism and urban unrest. Its ultimate achievements are hard to measure. They were developments attempting to influence urban decline and deprivation which were driven by economic forces, often emanating from far away. They helped to produce new ways of thinking about policy. Amongst officials they stimulated a quest for new ways of targeting policies upon specific areas (Hambleton, 1978). Amongst the young radicals who were drawn, particularly through CDP, into engagement with public policy, they contributed to the emergence of what came to be called the 'new urban left' (Gyford, 1985) which later set out to have an impact upon local government. They led on to local initiatives with a particular concern about economic policies at the local level, dividing into Leftist initiatives which saw local government as a key actor and a Conservative view that local power needed to be over-ridden by centrally controlled special agencies. The urban programme started a form of response to deprivation in which government expenditures have been modest but which have been claimed to be effectively targeted. An alternative view, which has been expressed over and over again from the initial statements of disillusion by the CDP teams onwards, is that they involve efforts to seek maximum publicity and kudos for the government from minimum expenditure (see Higgins et al., 1983, for a discussion of the various views).

Conclusions

Since the Labour verdict on the previous Conservative rule was that there had been '13 wasted years' it can hardly complain that the verdict of many people on its period of rule has been (in the words used in the title of Clive Ponting's book) that there had been a 'breach of promise'. Such a verdict is probably most usually applied to the failures in economic and industrial policy. But, as was shown in the introduction, it was also applied to social policy.

In social policy this was a government that aspired to do much. Its continuing economic difficulties limited what it achieved. The spate of diary writing by politicians in this period suggests that it was a government very influenced by civil servants who argued that some of its policies were impractical. Its policy innovations were therefore muted and cautious. They were also sometimes contradictory, as was suggested in the area of social security.

Yet it was also a government that continued to move social policy forward - the key examples of this being earnings-related benefits and comprehensive education. It was a more generous spender on social policy than the government which preceded it. But the record of its Conservative successor was in turn probably rather more generous than its.

Its mixed performance seemed inevitably to depend to some extent upon personalities. But it was also the case that in the early part of the period, the social policy ministries remained comparatively low in status, as in the 1951-64 governments. Initially Wilson dealt with this by appointing a minister to exercise broad overall supervision on some of the key issues. Later, he recognised that something more was needed and Richard Crossman was given responsibility for a combined Department of Health and Social Security.

It is important to note that 1964-70 was still a period when a Labour government could clearly aspire to use increments of growth for social policy ends, along the lines advocated in an influential book by one of the members of that government (Crosland, 1956). Indeed it was prepared to increase expenditure a little more than that. The idea that there was a 'crisis' for social policy expenditure still lay in the future.

6   The Conservative Government 1970-74

Introduction

When Harold Wilson called a general election in June 1970, Labour was well ahead in the opinion polls. The Conservatives, who had been led by Edward Heath since 1965, seemed unprepared for office. Wilson and his colleagues campaigned as the new natural party of government, attempting to frighten the electorate off Tory extremism. This involved exploiting evidence that the latter seemed to be developing new Right-wing policies. Nevertheless, the Conservatives won an election in which turnout was down and support for the Liberals a little reduced. They won 46.4 per cent of the total vote to Labour's 43.0 per cent. In the new House of Commons of 630 members the Conservatives had 330 members, Labour 287 and the other parties 13. Ulster Unionists could just be counted as still loyal to the Conservatives at this stage.

The Heath government of 1970-74 has yet to receive careful study. Quite apart from the fact that detailed historical work normally occurs only after the release of records, 30 years on, the events of these four years, which were in many respects a crucial transitional period in British post-war political history, have not received the scrutiny already devoted to the Thatcher era. Equally, whilst the financial crisis faced by the succeeding Labour government has received considerable attention, the events and policies of the Heath era, which laid some of the foundations for that crisis, have not yet been examined carefully. Perhaps the contrast arises partly because the Conservatives have written little about their experiences in this government whilst there has been an extensive outpouring of diaries and autobiographies from the Labour participants in the later events.

The economic record of the Heath government is a curious one. A conference held at Selsdon Park Hotel in early 1970, designed to establish policy for the forthcoming election, seemed to establish a determination to move the Conservatives sharply to the Right. There was a commitment to privatisation and an attack on Labour support for 'lame-duck' enterprises. 'Selsdon Man' was portrayed as a radical-Right bogy, by the media as well as by the Labour Party, in the way Thatcherism came to be in the 1980s. Yet, in the face of rising unemployment in 1971 and 1972 - in many ways the product of the previous Labour Chancellor's commitment to austere fiscal policies - the Conservative government shifted ground hurriedly. It showed itself only too willing to mount rescue operations for ailing industries and it allowed public expenditure to rise sharply. The combination of an initial relaxed approach to price and wage controls (based upon a belief that they should occur naturally through market processes) and the introduction of tax cuts to stimulate 'enterprise', followed soon by the panicky abandonment of expenditure restraints helped to create a combination of unemployment and inflation ('stagflation') which was to characterise much of the 1970s.

The Conservatives' 'U-turn' on fiscal policy was then followed by a similar reversal of policy on control of the economy as a whole. In Morgan's words 'the government now went from the extreme of non-intervention to new heights of corporatism' (Morgan, 1990, p.323). The government tried to develop corporatist industrial policies in collaboration with the Confederation of British Industry and the Trades Union Congress. Most importantly it sought to bring stagflation under control through strict statutory incomes policies. In attempting the latter it was handicapped by its initial hostility to the trade unions, and particularly by its imposition of legislation upon them aimed at curbing unofficial industrial action. It had not therefore laid the ground very well for a partnership with the trade union movement; this proved to be its undoing when its later inflexible approach to wage control led it into a confrontation with the National Union of Mineworkers. A more nimble politician than Edward Heath might have avoided getting himself into a situation in which he fought, and just lost, a general election conducted, with industry reduced by power shortages to a three day week, around the theme 'who runs Britain'. However, as will be seen - the conclusion the Labour Party drew from that experience - that it had a better way to cope with industrial relations, proved illusory. Rather more significant was the lesson the Conservative Right learned that it had to pay rather more attention to tactics before getting into conflict with a group of workers like the miners.

Where did social policy figure in all this? Labour thought it detected in 'Selsdon Man' a new hard line. The initial cuts in public expenditure seemed to confirm this. Labour focused in particular upon cuts in the availability of milk for school children, seeing an opportunity to attack a politician newly risen to Cabinet rank at the Department of Education as

'Thatcher the milk snatcher'. Yet once the initial hard-line fiscal policy was relaxed, social policy expenditure leapt ahead. Raison, in his account of Conservative social policies (Raison, 1990) is in no doubt that the Selsdon Man label never really fitted Tory social policy at this time. Even Margaret Thatcher's impact upon education policy as a whole was one of managing the consensus like her 1950s predecessors. Apart from the rather exaggerated notoriety she acquired as 'the milk snatcher', her record at the Department of Education was distinguished by the following:

> the increase of the school leaving age to 16 in 1973 (a measure postponed in Labour's economic crisis of 1968);

> the championing of pre-school education, where she aimed for a substantial increase;

> despite the fact that she repealed the circular requiring authorities to develop comprehensive schemes, during her time at the Department the number of pupils in such schools in England and Wales increased from about 35 to nearly 60 per cent;

> she published a White Paper on education policy in 1972 subtitled 'A Framework for Expansion' and, as has already been said, she increased education spending significantly more than her Labour predecessors.

Hugo Young (1989, pp.73-4) suggests that Thatcher was misled into her decision to cut school milk by her officials in an effort to release resources for other purposes, and came to regret it bitterly. Heclo and Wildavsky cite her as an example of a minister fighting her corner and 'commending herself to a client audience by citing increased spending' (1974, pp.135-6). Whatever Margaret Thatcher may have become as Prime Minister, she seems to have been a classic example of an Education Minister firmly in the control of her civil servants.

If we look at this era in terms of Conservative party personalities, an equally curious case study is provided by Sir Keith Joseph. When he became one of Thatcherism's leading ideologists later in the decade, he was prepared to publicly 'confess' that he had been in error as Secretary of State for Social Services in the Heath government when he had fought for more money for his department and presided over social policy innovations. Contrary to popular prejudices, politicians do learn, and the Heath era was perhaps a seminal period in the development of Margaret

Thatcher and Keith Joseph.

However, to conceptualise Conservative social policy at this period in terms of a contrast between the promise (or threat) of Selsdon Man on the one hand, and continuity with the Conservative post-war past on the other, is to oversimplify presentation of this interesting period in the evolution of policy. Raison shows that a considerable amount of thinking was going on within the party, and within the groups relating to it. In the centre of much of this was a search for ways of (what has subsequently come to be called) 'targeting' social policy. In social security there was an interest in negative income tax as an alternative to insurance, and a strong commitment to strengthening the private pensions industry. In 1965 Geoffrey Howe published, through the Conservative Political Centre, a pamphlet significantly entitled 'In Place of Beveridge'. Ways of altering the funding of the health service were being explored, with 'hotel' charges for in-patients, which had been suggested in Thorney-croft's package of cuts in 1957 (see Chapter 4), emerging again as one of the favourite ideas. The sale of council houses was being championed and new approaches to housing subsidy were being explored. The first two of the Black Papers challenging the progressive consensus in education were published in 1969 (Cox and Dyson, 1969a, 1969b).

By contrast, the Conservatives' election manifesto was full of promises to do better than Labour had done in social policy. This was set out in ways which linked Labour's social policy record with its poor economic record. It was clearly part of the orthodoxy for both parties at this time that social policy growth depended upon economic growth.

The expenditure record of the Heath government demonstrates a pattern of social policy expenditure growth which stands comparison with both the Labour government which preceded and the one which followed it. Data of this kind are difficult to analyse over the long run, being confused by administrative changes, definitional changes and, sometimes by an explicit desire by our political leaders to make trend comparisons difficult. Richard Rose's analysis in *Do Parties Make a Difference?* (1984) finds a considerable amount of evidence in the public expenditure continuities between the late 1950s and the early 1970s for an answer of 'no' to the question in his title. His data suggests that public expenditure grew faster under Heath than under Wilson's 1964-70 government. Walker reaches broadly similar conclusions (Walker, ed., 1982, p.30). He shows an expenditure growth rate for social policy of 6.8 per cent per annum, in comparison with 5.9 per cent in 1964-70. Within his data set health (7.1 per cent) and housing expenditure (19.9 per cent) show significantly greater rates of growth, with education (4.0 per cent) and social security

(3.1 per cent) showing lower annual growth rates under the Heath government. The housing figure is rather misleading, however, as there was a shift in housing support from the social security to the housing account with the introduction of a universal rebate and allowance system for tenants. It was in any case an increase within a much smaller budget: that for housing was only half that for education or health. In the 1980s further changes to the housing support system will be seen to produce a shift the opposite way, from housing to social security, in the national expenditure accounts.

The Heath government experienced a very similar growth rate of GDP to that of the Wilson government. This meant that it, too, was increasing social expenditure faster than the rate of economic growth. The great dividing point between high and lower public expenditure growth came about two years into the life of the succeeding Labour government.

However, comparison of public expenditure programmes has already been identified as difficult. It is only recently that experts on the analysis of social policy have begun to give careful attention to the factors which affect expenditure growth (see, in particular, Heald, 1983; Hills, 1990). They have shown how fundamentally important underlying demographic trends are in producing pressures upon expenditure which are politically very difficult to resist. Britain's ageing population has produced a strong and intensifying upward pressure, particularly on the social security and the health care budgets since the Second World War. But these analyses show two other strong influences upon social policy expenditure. One of these is the rising cost of inputs to the social services, particularly salaries. The other is the extent to which economic adversity, and particularly unemployment, increases needs. The 'stagflation' of the early and mid-1970s clearly exacerbated both these pressures. In this context Heath's attempted 'way out' involving statutory incomes policies had the effect of ensuring that public servants would share in wage growth triggered by inflation.

Analysis of the social policies of the Heath government in terms of expenditure figures, whilst confirming Raison's (1990) account of continuity, may obscure other things which were happening. In fact the Heath era was very important as a period of exploration of new policy options which were to come to fruition later. In the fields of social security and housing (and particularly where these two interact), there were developments which have proved of enormous importance for the future of British social policy. The roots of these changes will be analysed carefully in separate sections below. In other areas - health, education, personal social services - there were few significant policy changes. However, in these areas the search for new institutional arrangements initiated by Wilson was continued under the leadership of another Prime Minister who has also been described as a 'civil servant manqué' and who was, even more than Wilson a believer in rational policy analysis techniques. This meant that there was extensive institutional reform both within and between departments, motivated at this time by a desire to make the public sector more efficient rather than by a desire to supplant it. Perhaps the subsequent disillusion with what could be achieved by reorganising local government and the health service, by developing planning systems for government departments and by encouraging cross-departmental thinking (through bodies like the Central Policy Review Staff set up by Heath) ultimately contributed to the fiercer anti-public sector thrust of Thatcherism. Hence, sections in the later part of this chapter will look further at some of the institutional changes of this era, inasmuch as they affected social policy.

Social Security: Looking for Ways to Extend Selectivity

Whilst the subtitle of this section draws attention to the search the Conservatives engaged in for ways of extending selectivity during this government, it would be wrong to suggest that all their activities could be summed up in this way. They extended pensions as a right to the small number of over eighties who had failed to get into the Beveridge scheme, and they lowered the qualifying age for widows' pensions. But these were comparatively low-cost concessions. Rather more important was the introduction of Attendance Allowance for disabled people in need of care.

But the important area of activity on the social security front concerned the development of contributory pensions and a new initiative on family benefits. On contributory pensions the Conservatives had to decide what, if anything, to do to carry forward the legislation which the Labour government had come so close to enacting. Their alternative stance was set out in their manifesto:

> We believe that everyone should have the opportunity of earning a pension related to their earnings. But, in contrast to the Labour Party, our view is that, for the great majority of people, this can and should be achieved through the improvement and expansion of occupational schemes....

They proposed a 'reserve earnings-related state scheme' from which it would be easy for contributors to private schemes to contract out. Their statement ended with a pledge which was rather more of a hostage to fortune:

Our proposals will be fair to those who are now old, and also fair to those now working. Under Labour's scheme their pension prospects would depend upon the willingness of future generations to pay an ever-increasing pensions bill through mounting taxation. Under our proposal, a growing part of the future cost of pensions will be met through genuine savings.

If that really implied a commitment to large current pension increases and the introduction of funding for state contributors, it implied a dangerous strategy which would impose substantial additional costs on workers in taxes for the former and in insurance contributions for the latter! Not surprisingly the government backed away from the first of these commitments. It did, however, extend the politically useful device of making earnings-related contributions the basis for all insurance benefits, getting away from Beveridge's flat-rate contributions scheme (which had already been partly undermined by the earlier Conservative graduated pensions legislation and by Labour's addition of earnings-related short-term benefits). Legislation for the new pensions scheme was enacted, but the government lost power before it could be implemented.

In any short account of pensions policies at this time it is quite difficult to separate Conservative and Labour policy makers' thinking about contributory pensions. Many Labour activists would have liked to see a universal contributory pension. In practice the existence of many satisfactory private schemes, including in particular schemes for public employees, made this an unrealistic aspiration. Either those already provided for would have had an additional scheme to support them (which, of course, they would initially have to pay extra for) or private schemes would have had to be compulsorily rolled up into a general scheme which would offer an inferior deal for many. Conservative activists, on the other hand, favoured keeping pensions under private control, supporting in the process a powerful and growing industry in which many insurance companies, banks and investment specialists were involved. For them the problem was how to fulfil a pledge to extend contributory pensions to the many poorer paid and less secure workers outside the existing private schemes. In Chapter 4 the Conservatives' first attempt at doing this was examined. It offered a very poor deal by comparison with Labour's schemes. What Sir Keith Joseph offered was

... that everyone should have the opportunity to have two pensions - a basic pension through the State scheme and an earnings-related pension through a satisfactory occupation scheme, or failing that, a State reserve scheme (House of Commons speech, 28 November 1972, col. 243, quoted in Ellis, 1989, p.42).

To achieve this he had to set up a mechanism for determining whether private schemes offered terms protecting contributors adequately. In the distinction between the scheme adopted by Sir Keith Joseph and the one eventually enacted by his Labour successor, Barbara Castle, a great deal was to hinge on the comparison between approved private schemes and the state scheme. Labour particularly identified women workers as disadvantaged by Sir Keith's approach. The same issue emerged again in the 1986 legislation in which the Conservatives weakened the Castle scheme.

The final point about this piece of abortive legislation is that this was the only attempt ever made in Britain to institute a 'funded' state pensions scheme. A Board of Management would have been set up, independent of the National Insurance fund and the Exchequer. Ellis reports that:

> ... the Government Actuary estimated that if reserve scheme membership proved constant at around 7 million... the annual income of the Fund would be around £300 million. By the end of the century some £7 billion would have accrued (Ellis, op. cit. p.41).

For those who like to speculate on what might have been: how would future governments have dealt with this publicly controlled fund? Would they have raided it to reduce public expenditure? (note the comment on this in the Crossman diaries reported in the last chapter). Or would a Labour government have conceivably recognised that it had acquired a device which could be used to extend social control over private enterprise?

Turning now to family benefits, it was shown in the last chapter how Labour was edging slowly towards eliminating the income tax-related allowance for children to fund instead the universal Family Allowance. A crucial aspect of this, which had not been tackled, was that the tax allowance covered the first child whilst Family Allowance only covered the second and subsequent children. Movement towards a new approach had been slow, and an alternative Treasury view had been advanced that there should be a means-tested allowance.

It was also shown that the Child Poverty Action Group (CPAG) had been disappointed with Labour's slow response. During the election campaign it had to face a difficult dilemma. It saw its main hope of progress to lie in securing Labour's backing for its ideas. However, it was committed to acting as an independent pressure group and, to stiffen the resolve of a future Labour Parliamentary party,it felt bound to attack the inadequacy of the Wilson government's policies to combat child poverty. It must be remembered, too, that it did this at a time when it was widely believed that Labour would win the next election. It also felt it important to try to persuade the Conservatives of the case for increasing Family Allowance by 'clawing back' tax allowances. It succeeded in securing a pledge from the then shadow Chancellor of the Exchequer, Iain Macleod, to do this.

Some of the Labour leadership, notably Richard Crossman, regarded CPAG's attack on Labour policies as a betrayal, and thought that the publication of evidence, during the election period, on the growth of poverty contributed to the election defeat. From CPAG's point of view the object of the campaign was not achieved at this time (but see Chapter 7 for a crucial later instalment to the story). The Conservatives' election manifesto indicated that they were likely to go in a different direction. It said:

> We will tackle the problem of family poverty and ensure that adequate family allowances go to those families that need them. A scheme based upon negative income tax would allow benefits to be related to family need; other families would benefit by reduced taxation.

The key to the Conservative response lies in the final words of those two sentences - emphases upon targeting and upon reduced taxation. Raison explains the rejection of the 'claw-back' approach by paraphrasing three reasons given by Sir Keith Joseph:

> First... family allowances gave no help for families with only one child - yet to bring in first children would take time and also add greatly to the cost of the scheme. Second, an increase in family allowance, whether or not taxed, could not be at a level which would give significant help to the... poorest of wage-earning households. And thirdly, the lowering of the standard rate income tax threshold by Labour meant that certain people who should be seen as in the category of family poverty were actually paying income tax and would therefore derive no benefit from family allowance after tax had been clawed back (Raison, 1990, pp.73-4).

The last point was particularly important and had indeed caused the previous Labour government to hold back. As Banting showed (1979) in his study of Labour's struggles with this issue, the lowering of the tax threshold (mainly as a result of difficulties in ensuring that tax allowances kept up with inflation) had systematically eroded what was a powerful idea when it was first floated earlier in the 1960s.

The Conservatives sought to attack this issue by two measures. One was the immediate production of a new benefit - Family Income Supplement. This idea was clearly taken off the 'shelves' of the Treasury, as the Labour Chancellor, James Callaghan, had mooted it in

1967. The other was a Green Paper (HMSO, Cmnd 5116, 1972) which proposed a scheme of 'tax credits' for *all* children. This would involve payments to parents (probably the mothers - though this provoked administrative opposition). The idea came under fire from all quarters. If it were to be introduced with no losers - that is, leaving existing gainers from Family Allowance and child tax allowance intact - it would be very expensive. In these circumstances it would be both less egalitarian and more expensive than the CPAG universal Family Allowance with its clawback proposal. If introduced in a more limited form it would entail extensive administrative reform with very little real gain for the poor.

The new Family Income Supplement (FIS) proposal, on the other hand, was taken forward. This was a means-tested benefit for which low-income wage earners with children could apply. Initially opposition to this measure mainly concentrated upon the argument that the government was subsidising low wages, in effect reintroducing the Speenhamland system of poor relief abolished in 1834. Writing at a distance of over 20 years, during which FIS and its successor Family Credit (FC) have grown in importance, that objection to the measure seems to have long disappeared. It might have been expected that the emergent free marketeers, opposed to wage subsidies, would join the egalitarians in attacking it. Perhaps they did not because, whilst the Speenhamland system could be seen as a direct measure to enable farmers to subsidise their own wage payments, in the complex labour market of today it would be difficult for an employer to ensure that a significant part of the labour force was subsidised in this way. Many of the lowest paid workers are not people with direct entitlements to this benefit, rather they are married women and young single people. Far from there being obvious situations in which specific employers deliberately encourage FIS/FC applications, take-up has been low and government campaigns have been necessary to try to assure people that they can get this benefit to support them in low-paid jobs. It is interesting to note that research on employers' awareness of means-tested benefit is on the Department of Social Security's research agenda at the time of writing this book.

However, taking a long view, the central issue about the introduction of FIS has been neither the 'Speenhamland' issue nor take-up, but the fact that by introducing this measure, together with means-tested support for low-income rent payers (which will be discussed further in the next section), the Heath government produced what has proved to be one of the most intractable problems for British social security - the 'poverty trap'. When Joseph worried that the low earners he wanted to help were already tax-payers (and it might be added also National Insurance contribution payers now faced by a graduated payment system), he refused to recognise that to add a means-tested benefit that would logically taper off as income rose would mean that the problem faced by an individual trying to lift him or herself out of poverty (an important aspiration in Joseph's philosophy) would be made more difficult. In the second reading debate on the legislation, Shirley Williams and others of her Labour colleagues pointed out the inconsistency between a concern about incentives expressed as a reason for lowering tax rates and the disregard of the same principle in relation to a means-tested benefit imposing 'at the absolute minimum ... a disincentive of 50 per cent' (Hansard, 10 November 1970, col.237). Her point was echoed by a Conservative, Sir Brandon Rhys Williams, who said 'The Secretary of State does not deny that this is putting people in poverty straight on to surtax rates' (ibid., col.284). A modest rise in income would result in more tax, a higher insurance payment and less FIS. If then, as a consequence of later legislation under the Heath government (see the next section), low-income people were in receipt of a rent rebate or allowance as well this problem would be even worse.

Hence, one of the most significant lasting 'achievements' of the Heath government was to institutionalise the 'poverty trap' (Field, 1972). Subsequent Conservative inspired means-test changes have made it worse, despite the fact that the party's discussions of social security acknowledge it as a problem. Perhaps this is partly because they regard it as a lesser evil than the 'unemployment trap' which arises when benefits for those in work may be higher than for those out of work.

Housing Policy: Continuity and Change

In their election manifesto the Conservatives returned to a theme which they had used with success against Labour in 1951. They asserted, in a section entitled 'Homes for All', that

> New drive and impetus is urgently needed to reverse the biggest decline in the housing programme for a quarter of a century. Labour has failed to honour its pledge to build 500,000 houses a year by 1970. It is scandalous that this year, as last year, fewer houses will be completed than in 1964 when Labour took over.

They went on, as might be expected, to give particular attention to the decline in the building of owner-occupied housing. However, they by no means ignored the public sector. They put as the first of their three objectives:

> To house the homeless, to concentrate on slum clearance and to provide better
> housing for those many families living without modern amenities.

Their achievement did not manage to match up to their promise; the
output of new houses continued to decline until 1974 when it was close
to 200,000. It must be remarked about both this government and its
predecessor that this was very much an era when the health of the
building industry was a reflection of the health of the economy as a
whole. It was an era when efforts to stimulate the economy, or more
significantly to prevent it from overheating, had a very direct impact upon
the building industry.

The element of continuity in housing policy is however very evident,
with a significant programme of both private and public building
continuing. Around 40 per cent of the houses built under the Heath
government were in the public sector, a rather higher percentage than
during the later years of the previous Labour government.

Continuity is similarly evident when public expenditure on housing is
examined (a point which comes out more strongly if the reader looks
ahead at the data for the Thatcher governments). Indeed, as suggested
above, housing expenditure increased much faster under Heath than under
Wilson's 1964-70 government. This is, however, a statistic to be read
with some care. The rapid inflation of this period, with land prices and
building costs rising particularly rapidly, pushed up the need for subsidies
for public sector building (see Malpass, 1990, p.130). Also, as pointed
out above, there is a peculiar area of confusion between housing
expenditure and social security expenditure arising from policy changes.

The final area of apparent continuity lies in the fact that the Conservatives, at this time, did not interfere with the existing Labour legislation to
control the rents of private accommodation. However, once again an
absence of legislative change may be misleading. First because, as was
seen in the last chapter, the 'fair rents' formula left a great deal to the
discretion of rent officers and rent assessment committees, who might be
expected to be sensitive both to changes in the parts of the market they
could not control and to changes in the political atmosphere. Second, the
Rent Acts left loopholes - for example the scope for 'licences to occupy'
as opposed to registered tenancies. Third, the government delayed
implementing the recommendation of the Francis Committee that
furnished tenancies should be brought into the controlled system.

On top of these came a new policy - the introduction of a system of rent
allowances for private-sector tenants. This was included within legislation

also concerning the public sector which will be discussed next. Whilst having no direct impact upon the system of rent control, it did introduce an alternative approach to the protection of tenants who could not afford market rents, am approach which was more compatible with the ideal that government should not interfere with markets, which was to assume greater significance in the late 1980s.

The major change in housing policy came with the 1972 Housing Finance Act. This was legislation which aimed to effect change gradually, hence its full impact was limited by Labour repeal in 1974. However, there must have been, at this time, a significant shift in the way the Department of the Environment thought about council house subsidy systems. Even though Labour modified those parts of the new policy it liked the least, it did not shift entirely away from it. A revolution in the funding of council housing was started which later Conservative governments effectively advanced in the 1980s.

The Housing Finance Act required rents for local authority tenants to move upwards towards 'fair rent' levels, as determined by a national system. The problematical nature of this concept has already been noted in the last chapter. Clearly what the government wanted was a sharp rise in public sector rents, using private rents as a comparator and bringing them close to market rents. It expected the general subsidy from central government to local authority housing to be phased out, except where there were particularly expensive developments (involving, for example, expensive land or costly slum clearance schemes). It planned the move to the new rent structure to occur gradually, and started by setting targets for individual authorities which would force rent rises by reducing subsidies.

In order to soften the impact of this change for low-income tenants, the government introduced a national rent rebate scheme, underpinned by government grants which would pay part of the cost for local authorities. This scheme, together with the rent allowances scheme for private tenants which accompanied it and which means-tested individuals in the same way, made further contributions to the 'poverty trap', discussed in the previous section. In fact, the poverty trap was not the only problem brought in by this new way of subsidising low income tenants. Many such individuals, if out of work, were obtaining help with their rents through the Supplementary Benefit scheme. Devices had to be worked out to prevent deliberate cost shifting between the local authorities and the central social security agency, other than that intended and budgeted for by central government. There was also a problem that some tenants were better off with support from one source, while others were better off seeking help from the other. The government made various, only partly successful, attempts at solving these problems. In the end further legislation was needed in 1983 and 1986, and even today there remain some problems of equity concerning the relationship between means-tested subsidies related to housing status and the social security system.

The Heath government took the first really clear steps towards transforming the British system of subsidy for low-income house-holders from one which concentrated upon subsidies for public tenants and rent control for private tenants to one which concentrates upon 'targeting' help to individuals by way of means tests. In doing so it generated a range of policy implementation problems and therefore a succession of further reforms designed to sort out the resultant muddle or advance the process (or both together, as has been the case since the mid-1980s).

At the same time, as stated in the earlier section, this government bequeathed to future generations the 'poverty trap' in a fairly chronic form because of its insistence on advancing two new family means tests at the same time. This can hardly be dismissed as carelessness based on ignorance of the effects of means testing since, as was shown above, the poverty trap effect had been pointed out in the second reading debate on the Family Income Supplement Bill. In the second reading debate on the Housing Finance Bill a number of members, including the Conservatives Sir Brandon Rees Williams and Ralph Howell, deplored the fact that the government was simply developing another means test without consider-ing how it fitted in with the existing ones.

Institutional Change under the Heath Government

It was noted in the last chapter that it was left to Edward Heath to complete the processes of institutional reform of local government and of the health service which were initiated by Wilson. As far as the former was concerned, the Conservatives deviated from the model favoured by the Royal Commission largely because of their commitments to the counties and smaller districts where much of their own political support lay. Otherwise they shared the general aspiration to create larger units, deemed to be able to offer a more efficient service. It was beginning to be recognised at this time that the system of local government finance and of grants to local government might also need revision.

The reform of the health service, like the reform of local government by the Heath administration, also needs noting as an institutional change in the spirit of the earlier consensus, with little hint of the problem its powers and its finance was to be perceived to be by a future Conservative government. A third 'district' tier was added to the larger areas in the structure as suggested by Crossman. A most complex consultative structure was set up, based upon elaborate advice from management consultants. Klein has described the plan as:

> a political exercise in trying to satisfy everyone and to reconcile conflicting policy aims: to promote managerial efficiency but also to satisfy the professions, to create an effective hierarchy for transmitting national policy but also to give scope to the managers at the periphery (Klein, 1989, p.99).

Klein's book, like this one, was written with the benefit of hindsight. Stresses in the system soon showed. Failure to confront the power of the professions soon came home to roost in a host of problems for Sir Keith Joseph's Labour successor, Barbara Castle, but it was the later Conservative governments which really took this new structure to pieces.

Edward Heath came to power very committed to reviewing the institutions of central government. In the 1960s the Plowden Committee (HMSO, Cmnd. 1432, 1961) had secured reforms in the system of expenditure control and the Fulton Committee (HMSO, Cmnd.3638, 1968) had suggested reforms to the structure of the civil service, but there remained concerns about the quality of advice directly available to the Prime Minister and the related issue of the extent of policy coordination between departments.

In October 1970 the Central Policy Review Staff (CPRS) was set up. This was a small unit (16 strong by autumn 1971) attached to the Cabinet Office, made up of a mixture of career civil servants and outsiders drawn from the business and academic worlds. These people served in CPRS on a temporary basis for around two years each (this description is drawn from Blackstone and Plowden, 1988, Chapters 1 and 2). CPRS was expected to have direct access to the Cabinet and to ministers and to carry out a mixture of large studies (with a strong emphasis on topics that cut across departmental boundaries) and shorter reviews of issues of the day. In general, it was expected to play a role in sensitising departments to the need to consider priorities carefully. Such a group was bound to be regarded with suspicion by many ministers and civil servants, and some of CPRS's interventions (particularly later in its history) attracted considerable criticism. Blackstone and Plowden say: 'Close links with, and the goodwill of, the Prime Minister of the day were always seen as important by the CPRS. When the goodwill finally ran out, the CPRS went with it' (ibid., p.45). CPRS enjoyed its honeymoon period with Heath. It was viewed with less enthusiasm by Wilson and Callaghan, who had their own separate and more directly political 'policy unit'.

Thatcher closed it down in 1983.

A Heathite reform of administration closely connected with CPRS was Programme Analysis and Review (PAR) set up in 1971. This venture, which did not last very long (see Gray and Jenkins, 1985, who suggest it was already in decline by 1974) involved the review of specific departmental programmes.

In the field of social policy probably the most important CPRS intervention was the setting up of a sequence of policy review exercises which became known as the 'Joint Approach to Social Policy' (JASP). This was initiated in 1972 but continued into the period of Labour rule. It played a role in the recognition, so important for social policy in the 1970s, of the need to give careful attention to the implications for 'outputs' of resource constraints. Ideally, it aimed to help with the identification of needs which should be given priority despite cutting exercises. It certainly worked hard at putting issues about family policy, female employment and child care on the agenda. It also seems to have played a role in the development (which will be charted further in later chapters) of the need to see social or community care as an essentially inter-departmental issue. Blackstone and Plowden, themselves ex-members of CPRS and sympathetic historians of the venture, are unsure about its contribution to social policy-making:

> On social policy and economic policy the CPRS's main contribution was to see the interrelationship between different parts of the jigsaw and to start its analysis with the needs of the citizen for social services (Blackstone and Plowden, 1988, p.199).

Employment Policy: A Significant Area of Institutional Change

Whilst the links between many of the institutional changes initiated by the Heath government and specific policies were comparatively indirect, there was one area where such a change was seen to be a launching pad for an important combination of social policy and economic policy changes. This was in the field of employment.

In much of Europe at this time policies were sought that would help to smooth out the trade cycle and its negative effects. Manpower policies were one such example. The tendency of the economy to 'overheat' and for inflation to accelerate was partly attributed to skilled manpower shortages. It was argued that 'active manpower policy' could involve the use of 'contra-cyclical' devices. A valuable form of public spending to get the economy out of the trough in the trade cycle could be measures to train the unemployed and boost public employment. This would then increase the supply of trained manpower and improve the public services infrastructure to ensure really effective growth once industry revived. In Europe, the Organisation for Economic Cooperation and Development (OECD) played an important role in the dissemination of these new ideas, with Sweden prominent amongst the innovating countries (see Bakke, 1969; OECD, 1964 and 1970; Mukherjee, 1972).

British governments had been slow to react to these new ideas. Fiscal policies remained the key regulators in the 1960s, with the efforts to shift the balance between the regions enhanced in various ways through taxation and subsidies. Some efforts were made in Britain to stimulate training in this period, with the development of a grant and levy system that aimed to secure public investment in training where firms were unwilling to train for their own needs. But the basic structure of the manpower policy system remained unchanged.

Edward Heath decided to restructure the public employment service as part of his government's efforts to make public administration more dynamic. A consultative document *People and Jobs* (Department of Employment, 1971a) declared that the employment service needed to be modernised. It argued that the Employment Exchanges were too identified with a limited service to the unemployed. A new active service needed to be created that would seek to have a real impact upon the functioning of the labour market. Responsibility for manpower policy was given, in 1973, to the specially created Manpower Services Commission (MSC), containing representatives of both sides of industry. The implementation of policy was taken out of the hands of the Department of Employment and given to two agencies, the Employment Services Agency and the Training Services Agency, which were to be separate accounting bodies, required to operate, as far as possible, on similar lines to private enterprise. While these new organisations were by and large staffed by civil servants from the Department of Employment, the government initiated an effective reappraisal of its role in manpower policy, and created a system that was to be very much more open to the development of new initiatives.

The reform of the employment service was justified in the following terms:

> For both social and economic reasons the country needs a public employment service which is positive and dynamic both in finding and filling jobs and as an instrument of wider labour market policies. The report sets the course for such an advance, and provides the basis for equipping the service to meet the demands which employer, worker and the requirements of public policy are likely to make on it in the 1970s (Department of Employment, 1971b, p.1101).

While institutional reorganisation, and the transformation of both the employment and the training functions that followed it, seemed to represent the British conversion to 'active manpower policy', by the 1970s the economic context had begun to change quite radically. In 1971-2 there was a trough in the trade cycle much more severe than any since the 1930s, and the modest 'peak' that followed it, in 1973-4, involved a relatively inadequate recovery in the level of unemployment. At the same time, as has been pointed out, there was high inflation. These twin problems continued for the next administration, with unemployment soon rising again. The new MSC became engaged in a very different activity to that for which it had been set up. It was required by the Labour governments to play a key role in developing special programmes for the unemployed. Its very flexibility, by comparison with a traditional ministry, made it quite effective at this task. When Margaret Thatcher came to power, after an initial doubt as to whether this essentially corporatist institution had a role in the new 'market' era, her government used it in the same way. Later, despite the fact that it was a pioneer example of a government agency (an administrative concept increasingly favoured), its original links with the corporatism of the Heath era caused the Thatcher axe to be brought down upon it.

Conclusions

The main social policy legacy of the Heath government, apart from the things which Thatcher and her supporters saw as errors to be avoided in future, was the early experiments in the extension of means tests for assistance to the working poor. These were applied as alternatives to the improvement of universal family allowances and to the provision of cheap housing. Together they created the 'poverty trap'. In the case of housing, the emergence of an approach to housing policy which would lead to the charging of market rents in the public sector and the lifting of restraints upon landlords in the private sector began a movement which, at the time of writing, is transforming housing provision, not just for the very poor but for many low income tenants. To the two measures described here the Thatcher governments added a policy which forced local authorities to sell many houses to their tenants at substantial discounts, a policy which the Heath government encouraged but did not impose upon local authorities.

As the last two sections have shown, there was also a range of administrative developments in the Heath era. As suggested in the introduction, however these were not necessarily new departures in social policy. Wilson, too, had seen himself as an institutional reformer. Since the early sixties there had been a belief in the need to modernise British institutions. Within both parties such a belief still put the state very much at the centre. It was, however, the limited achievements of these reforms and particularly the sense - growing in the Heath era but coming to a head under his Labour successors - that Britain had deeper problems, believed to be rooted in her economy rather than in her system of government per se - that created a search for very different kinds of reforms in which a very different role would be given to the state in the 1980s.

But first it is important to give a considerable amount of attention, in the next chapter, to two further Labour governments, even more racked by economic problems, which nevertheless sought to have an impact on social policy, carrying forward and trying to compensate for the limited achievements of the 1964-70 Labour regime.

7   The Labour Governments 1974-79

Introduction

Edward Heath's bid to win electoral support in February 1974, in the middle of his battle with the striking miners, was unsuccessful. Yet the election result was inconclusive. The Conservatives just won the highest proportion of the votes (37.9 per cent) but got only 297 seats. Labour gained 37.1 per cent of the votes and 301 seats. The Liberals won 14 seats. By this time the Conservatives could no longer depend upon the support of Unionists in Northern Ireland. There were 12 members from that country, nearly all Unionists of some variety. Finally there were 11 other members, 7 of whom were Scottish Nationalists. Heath made an initial bid to hold on to power, but eventually Harold Wilson formed another Labour administration.

The new government held on for over seven months, settling the miners' strike on terms favourable to the strikers and enacting a budget which increased taxation but also significantly increased benefits and social expenditure. It committed itself to replacing Heath's ill-fated experiment with incomes policy by what became known as the 'social contract', under which unions agreed to pay restraint in return for policies which would address the need to enhance the social wage through increased social policy spending and progressive taxation. There was a commitment to increase pensions in line with increases in earnings or prices (whichever was higher) and to increase short-term insurance benefits in line with prices. Meanwhile, a device adopted by Heath as part of a statutory incomes policy, to allow 'threshold' pay increases automatically as the cost of living rose, was left to complete its year of operation until October 1974. Hence the inflation which Heath had been attempting to control rose rapidly at this time.

The Conservatives were reluctant to provoke a further election immediately. Eventually Wilson decided to try to secure a proper mandate. There was a further election on 10 October 1974 when Labour succeeded in improving its position, but only narrowly. This time it achieved the highest proportion of the votes cast (39.2 per cent) and won 319 seats. The Conservatives secured 36.7 per cent of the votes and 277 seats. But there were 39 other MPs, so that once Labour started to lose by-elections, it needed to turn to some of the minor parties to retain power. By the end of 1976 it had lost three seats to the Conservatives; it was to lose four more (all but one to the Conservatives) before it eventually went to the country again. There were also some Labour defections, two of them to the newly formed Scottish Labour Party and one to the Conservatives (a former Cabinet Minister, Reg Prentice, in October 1977). After Wilson retired, to be replaced by James Callaghan in April 1976, Labour's hold on power began to become increasingly tenuous.

The unstable political position of the Labour government was reinforced by a succession of economic difficulties. As suggested above, the initial period of Labour rule was characterised by rapid inflation (but a reduction in unemployment), generated first by the legacy of Heath's policies and then fuelled by the dramatic rise in oil prices. The oil price shock came just before Britain could benefit as a significant oil producer in its own right. It had a disruptive effect upon the world economy, and the weakness of the British economy made it particularly vulnerable. Labour's initial response of maintaining a relaxed stance on individual income growth and increasing public expenditure is seen alternatively as a bold attempt to respond to the oil price rise by countering its deflationary effects (Ormerod in Bosanquet and Townsend, 1980, pp.49-50), or as an unrealistic attempt to adopt policies incompatible with those of Britain's more powerful trading partners (Dell, 1991, Chapter 6).

There is no point in joining the argument here. What is clear, even a severe critic of the policy like Dell acknowledges this, is that it would have been politically very difficult for the Labour government to have behaved very differently in its first year of rule. It lacked a clear majority. It was also deeply divided internally. In particular it had to resolve its internal wrangling over British membership of the European Economic Community, which it eventually did by way of the device of a referendum in which members of the Cabinet openly campaigned on opposite sides. This matter was resolved with a strong vote for staying in Europe in June 1975. Perhaps most important of all it had to manage its relationship with the Trade Unions, who had fought Heath on both incomes policy and trade union legislation and had also successfully opposed the 1964-70 Labour government on the latter. The 'social contract' was a vague understanding (which it is easy for writers from Labour's Right Wing, like Edmund Dell, to be sarcastic about in retrospect) but a necessary device which enabled the government to cope politically in its first few months.

Social policy was initially the beneficiary of the compromise described above. The social contract implied social policy progress. The Labour Left had, during the Heath years, engaged in a disillusioned debate about the lack of progress in social policy (as well as in other areas of policy where socialist commitments were felt to be relevant). New initiatives were demanded, particularly a resolution of the long running sagas of pensions and child support policy as well as a stronger line in support of the National Health Service. A strong Left-inclined minister was selected by Wilson to carry these initiatives forward in the Department of Health and Social Security - Barbara Castle. There was also a strong desire to see effective action against those local authorities which were dragging their feet on comprehensive education, though that policy did not have the serious cost implications of the initiatives required of Barbara Castle.

Hence the 1974-79 period of Labour rule can be seen as one in which there was an initial flurry of action on social policy. That was followed by a period of public expenditure cuts as the government changed course to respond to the crisis of inflation which confronted it. There is an important sense in which the autumn of 1975 can be seen as a watershed in the history of British social policy. In the early part of the year the new pensions scheme and the replacement of family allowances by child benefit were successfully passed through Parliament. In the middle of the year the Chancellor received trade union agreement to a very tight limitation on wage increases, threatening statutory controls if they did not agree. At the same time he began to impose public expenditure cuts on his colleagues. The system of 'cash limiting' departmental expenditure, forcing most expenditure programmes to stay within pre-determined budgets, which has since come to be a standard procedure, began to be imposed. There were also worries about the balance of payments, and some international support was secured in the later part of the year. Hence, to adapt the words Anthony Crosland applied to local government in 1975, the 'party' was over for social policy. In 1976, after Callaghan had succeeded Wilson as Prime Minister, the crisis intensified. When Britain was forced to borrow from the International Monetary Fund at the end of that year, one of the conditions of the loan was the acceptance of severe public expenditure restraints.

While it may be convenient for some to blame Callaghan or, more likely, the International Monetary Fund for the collapse of Labour's dreams, it is clear that the collapse had begun the year before. Moreover, as has been suggested in referring to some of the harsher judgements on this government (such as Dell's) there is a view that for both economic and political reasons the 1974 to 1979 Labour regime was never in a position to be an effective innovator in social policy. This author's preference is for seeing Barbara Castle's social security measures as a brave attempt to carry forward reforms in social policy that her ministerial predecessors in the 1960s had failed to enact.

After that the story of social policy in this period is one of trying to hold on to traditional policies in the face of a squeeze between growing demands on the one hand and falling resources on the other. Amongst the growing demands were the poverty and deprivation, which were consequences of the rising unemployment which inevitably followed the deflationary measures.

Trends in public expenditure have been given increasingly careful attention by academic analysts in recent years. To bring out clearly the very peculiar character of the period this chapter is concerned with, it is useful to draw upon two analyses of social policy expenditure trends, one written in 1980 (Bosanquet, in Bosanquet and Townsend eds., 1980) comparing the 1974-79 government with its predecessors, the other written in 1989 (Le Grand, in Hills ed., 1990) comparing the 1974-79 government with the first nine years of Thatcherism.

Bosanquet shows rates of increases in expenditure on social services which are extraordinarily similar for 1959-64, 1964-70 and 1970-74, of around 5 per cent per annum (Bosanquet, p.11). Note that this slightly differs from Walker's analysis, quoted in the last two chapters, which suggests a tendency for the increase in each of these periods to be slightly higher than in the previous one. It does, however, further support Rose's analysis in *Do Parties Make a Difference?* (Rose, 1984). Then Bosanquet's sequence of figures for the next four financial years make extraordinary reading. Table 7.1 sets them out, with his figures for 1970-74 included for comparative purposes.

Le Grand (in Hills ed., 1990), using similar data but using different definitions, comes up with a set of figures which bring out the peculiarity of 1974-75 even more sharply. His estimate of social policy expenditure growth for that year is 13.3 per cent. That is followed by 2.5 per cent for 1975-76, 3.7 per cent for 1976-77, minus 4.7 per cent for 1977-78 and then 1.5 per cent for 1978-79 (the year not quoted here from Bosanquet's analysis because it was only an estimate). Growth in the early years of the Thatcher governments settled at only just over 1 per cent until 1982-83, after which we see a more varied up and down pattern not unconnected with the timing of elections. But that is to run ahead to the subject of the next chapter. The book from which Le Grand's data are drawn contains a great deal of careful analysis of the trends in individual services. Clearly, as Bosanquet's figures suggest, housing expenditure was the easiest to manipulate quickly (tenants might rightly say 'erratic-ally'), whilst social security shows a pattern influenced, in the early period, by the commitment to indexing at a time of high inflation and, at the end of the period, by the introduction of child benefit and the rise of unemployment.

Table 7.1   Rates of increase in expenditure 1970-78 (at constant prices)

Year all	social services	social security	education	health	housing
1970-74	5.0	3.0	6.3	4.3	7.4
1974-75	9.0	6.9	0.4	1.0	44.1
1975-76	2.1	8.3	1.8	3.2	-11.7
1976-77	1.0	2.9	- 0.3	0.8	-1.0
1977-78	- 0.9	3.6	- 3.6	0.8	- 9.4

Derived by Bosanquet from Public Expenditure White Papers

Some economic commentators have portrayed the economic policies of the Chancellor of the Exchequer, Dennis Healey, as the end of the Keynesian era and the beginning of 'monetarism', with 1975 or 1976 as the crucial threshold. In observing the sharp 'break point' in the rate of growth of social expenditure at that time, it may equally be argued that this was the critical change point for social policy. However, that does not mean that this should necessarily be seen as the beginning of the Thatcher era.

There is an important distinction to be drawn between a powerless Labour government desperately seeking to preserve the ideals it stood for and Thatcher committing herself cheerfully to butchering social expendi-ture, even if what actually happened was not remarkably different. Labour's very success in acting against its own instincts in the interests of international financial respectability eventually brought the government down in the face of rising unemployment. The hostility of its own natural supporters, particularly in the public sector unions, generated the demoralising 'winter of discontent' of 1978-79, when uncleared rubbish and (exceptionally) unburied corpses provided marvellous election propaganda for the Conservatives. It reinforced the rationale for a New Right attack upon public social services and upon the providers of those services.

Meanwhile, the rest of this chapter will examine two areas of social policy where Labour, between 1974 and 1979, continued to try to move forward in ways compatible with its traditional commitments - social security and health (including personal social services) - , and two areas where its 'progress' was more uncertain - housing and education. Contrasting these two throws light upon the politics of this period, and on the strength of the new forces gaining confidence in the land. In conformity with the general policy in this book to be selective and to focus on significant political events, employment services will not be discussed. In the last chapter some attention was given to the setting up of the Manpower Services Commission. There it was pointed out that this provided a useful device for the rapid deployment of ad hoc responses to rising unemployment. That sums up employment policy over the period 1974-79. The absence of any alternative response left Labour - ruling a country with well over a million unemployed - vulnerable to a Conservative charge, proclaimed in posters all across the land in 1979, that 'Labour is not Working'. There was, in fact, worse to come! But that issue belongs to the next chapter.

Innovations in Social Security

Barbara Castle was Secretary of State responsible for the vast Department of Health and Social Security throughout Harold Wilson's term as Premier between spring 1974 and spring 1976. During that period she steered two crucial social security measures - on pensions and on child benefit - through Parliament, ably assisted in this work by one of her Ministers of State, Brian O'Malley. She retired to the backbenches when Wilson did, and at about the same time Brian O'Malley died prematurely. Castle's successor was David Ennals.

Our view of the Castle era is enriched, obviously not impartially, by her lively diaries (Castle, 1990). Ennals has so far left no such record, but the most important political processes occurring in social security during his term of office have been informatively discussed in a book by the then Chairman of the Supplementary Benefits Commission (Donnison, 1982). It should be added that the review of the supplementary benefits system which occurred at that time has been the only policy-making process in social policy at central government level that the present author has been able to observe from a partly 'inside track'. It is hoped that these factors do not lead to an over-emphasis upon social security policy-making at this time, but it is felt to be a particularly revealing set of events for the analysis contained in this book as a whole.

The measure to which least attention will be given here was arguably, at least in terms of its long-term implications, the most important of the three measures. As far as earnings-related pensions were concerned, there was already a measure on the statute book waiting to be implemented. Barbara Castle seemed initially only to have to decide whether to proceed with it in its entirety or modify it slightly. She decided that it was too flawed for either of these courses of action. From her point of view its weakness was that it was very much an inferior 'reserve' scheme. She wanted one which would provide a model for private schemes, enabling any private pension scheme to be refused approval if it was not of the same standard. One important way she set out to improve on Joseph's scheme was to offer a better deal for women, by provisions which compensated them for periods out of the labour market because of 'home responsibilities', by ensuring that benefits were based upon the best 20 years of a working life rather than the whole of it and by enabling state earnings-related pensions (SERPS as they came to be called) to be inherited by widows.

To achieve these changes Barbara Castle risked Parliamentary difficulties during the 'short Parliament' when Labour lacked an overall majority. In July 1974 she survived Parliamentary censure for withdrawing the Joseph scheme in July 1974, by a majority of two. New legislation was prepared and presented to Parliament in March 1975. This became law in August of that year and went into operation (which meant, in effect, only the beginning of a long period of accumulation of contributions to yield benefits many years later) in 1978. At the end of his monograph on this subject Ellis observes 'For the first time in twenty years pensions and their future were off the political agenda' (Ellis, 1989, p.58). He might have added 'only until 1984 when Norman Fowler started questioning whether the nation could afford SERPS'.

In its February 1974 manifesto the Labour party pledged itself to provide 'a new system of CHILD CASH ALLOWANCES [its capitals] for every child, including the first, payable to the mother'. A similar pledge appeared in the October manifesto. Barbara Castle's diaries report efforts by the Chancellor to persuade her on more than one occasion to delay legislation on this issue (Castle, 1990, p.501 and p.510). Her resistance was probably strengthened by the knowledge that she had clear Trades Union Congress support for the measure, in a sense making it an element in the 'social contract'. The necessary legislation was introduced in May 1975 and became law in August. It involved the replacement of the existing Family Allowance and child tax allowances by a child benefit payable for each child *including the first.*

However, there were flaws: the legislation did not contain a commitment on the amounts of benefit or on a starting date. In his budget of April 1975 the Chancellor announced a starting date of April 1977. A 'child interim benefit' was offered, one year earlier, of the modest sum of £1.50 for the first child of single-parent families.

In April 1976, as pointed out above, Wilson was replaced by Callaghan and Castle left office. Callaghan's hostility to a measure of this kind had been evident when he was Chancellor eight years previously (see Chapter 5). Within weeks of his succession, the new Secretary of State, David Ennals, announced on 25 May that the child benefit scheme was to be sacrificed to the need for public expenditure cuts. 'On 17th June', to quote from McCarthy's detailed account of the events which followed, *'New Society*, in an article perhaps unprecedented in the recent history of social policy, published a detailed account of the Cabinet's volte-face on child benefits based upon classified information, including secret Cabinet minutes, leaked to Frank Field, by an undisclosed source' (McCarthy, 1986, p.269).

Frank Field was the Director of the Child Poverty Action Group (CPAG). It was a measure of the lessons CPAG had learnt from the unhappy experience of the 1970 election that the group had gone to considerable lengths to build up a relationship with the trade union movement. Some of the unions and CPAG had worked together to get the original commitment to child benefit into the manifesto and to keep the issue on the agenda, the unions were now prepared to challenge the government on this decision. A 'Child Benefits Now' campaign was set up which secured a climb down on the part of the government, enabling the measure to be implemented in 1978.

The flavour of Callaghan's view, and probably that of Michael Cocks, the Chief Whip (who was alleged to have taken soundings on the issue), is set out in Dennis Healey, the Chancellor's, autobiography in typically brusque terms:

> It was he [Callaghan] who first realised that Child Benefit...might cost us male votes because it would mean a switch from the wallet to the handbag... We finally introduced Child Benefit in 1978. I believe it had the effect Jim feared; although that year saw the biggest increase in real family income for a long

time, the Labour Party failed to reap the full political benefit, since working men did not find the increase fully reflected in their own weekly pay packets (Healey, 1990, pp.448-9).

It is a measure of the British trade union movement's shift away from such a simplistic male chauvinist stance that the second of the 1974-79 government's two significant social policy innovations reached implementation.

The Treasury's preoccupation with social security costs, after the early months of the Labour government, forms a fitting introduction to the last of the issues to be discussed in this section. Since it was brought within the social security ministry in 1966, the means-tested Supplementary Benefit part of the social security system had involved a Commission headed by a full-time chairman. This body had two duties. One was to supervise the discretionary parts of the Supplementary Benefit system and to advise staff on how to exercise their powers. The other was to advise the ministry on supplementary benefits policy. The latter function had been exercised in a comparatively private and low-key way, with public statements from the Commission being largely defences against attack from the pressure groups.

In 1975 Barbara Castle appointed a new chairman, David Donnison, who was given a rather more active brief: to return to the old National Assistance Board practice of making an annual report in which to bring concerns about policy to the attention of the government and public. The private understanding between Barbara Castle and David Donnison was rather stronger than that. Donnison subsequently wrote:

> I had no formula to bring to the job - only a feeling that social assistance had been allowed to run on without any major shake up since 1948, and that times had changed since then. I had seen enough to know that the scheme was growing increasingly unmanageable. But to get any changes we would need the Secretary of State's support and a way of presenting uncensored ideas to the public and provoking a debate (Donnison, 1982, p.25).

He set out to do this by speaking out on issues and by ensuring that he secured regular meetings with field level staff, and with claimants and their advocates.

In 1976, Donnison secured departmental approval for a review of the Supplementary Benefit scheme, after an outspoken Annual Report making a case for it. This was to be a departmental venture, but Donnison was allowed to participate; the process of consultation and feedback of conclusions was to be a public one (see Donnison, op. cit., and Walker, 1983, for more details of the arrangements). This review nurtured wide expectations, particularly amongst the pressure groups - of which the CPAG was the most prominent - which had become known as the 'poverty lobby'. These expectations were to be frustrated by two things. One was that the review was solely of Supplementary Benefit, a serious disadvantage to many in the poverty lobby who saw the growth of means testing as the principal current problem in British social security (Lister, 1975, 1977). The second was that there was another party to the review process - the Treasury - which expected it to be a nil cost review. The poverty lobby's reaction to this is best expressed in another pamphlet Lister produced when the review team issued its initial conclusions for consultation, *The No-Cost No-Benefit Review* (Lister, 1979).

Despite these drawbacks, Donnison worked very hard to try to secure credibility for the review. His stance was that the British social security scheme had now entered an era where means testing was bound to play a central role (Donnison, 1977, 1979). It was therefore important to strengthen the rule-based rights within the scheme and to simplify it so that entitlements would become less ambiguous. As far as the nil cost constraint was concerned, he urged that simplification could bring savings, particularly in administrative costs, which then could be used to improve benefits.

The review report charted the way in which discretionary payments had grown throughout the life of the scheme. It was suggested that rules about entitlements to them would both advance 'rights' and stabilise costs. Perhaps the most original of the proposals to come out of the review was a suggestion that, instead of discretionary payments for clothing replacements, claimants who remained on benefit for a long while should receive regular automatic lump sums. Otherwise the aim was to itemise exceptional needs.

The review also looked at the muddle, referred to in the last chapter as the so-called 'better-off problem' - arising from the fact that some low income people's housing costs were met within the Supplementary Benefit scheme whilst others received help from local authority administered rent rebates and allowances. Individuals often faced dilemmas about which option offered them the best deal. Rationalisation was urged through the development of a single housing support scheme. However, as this would depend upon collaboration between the Department of Health and Social Security and the Department of the Environment, it was beyond the review team's brief.

Whilst these ideas were being considered by the government, it fell from power. The incoming Conservatives acted upon the suggestions of the review, but left out the proposal for regular lump sums. They also took action to deal with the housing costs problem. What they did on these two issues proved no more satisfactory for them than for their critics. Hence the subject of further extensive changes to means-tested social security benefits will arise again in the next chapter.

Except as a demonstration project in open government, this particular episode has to be regarded as something of a failure. Hopes were raised which, even if a change of government had not intervened, would surely have been shattered. The agenda was fixed in a narrow way at the outset. Perhaps again, like the events surrounding child benefit in 1970, it contributed to the political education of the poverty lobby, steeling it to face an even more impotent era in the 1980s. But that is not much consolation for people whose ideals of a return to a system of social security in which means tests would play a much less significant role had received a severe battering.

One important footnote to this activity was that it occurred at a time when agitation about the abuse of benefits systems by claimants was receiving increasing attention. Press campaigns on this issue had begun during the Heath government, and an official committee had investigated the issue (Fisher Committee, Cmnd.5228, 1973). The Right-wing press brought the issue to the boil again under Labour (see Deacon, 1978; Golding and Middleton, 1982). Clearly Donnison saw public hostility to some categories of claimants as making it more difficult to persuade the government to put additional money into Supplementary Benefit. It certainly seemed to be the case that at a time when family poverty was growing, with rising unemployment and increasing numbers of one-parent families, a body of opinion in 'Middle England' (Donnison, 1979, p.152) saw the welfare state as over-indulgent to some groups. This was one of the ways in which Labour's commitment to welfare may have become, to some degree, an electoral disadvantage at this time.

Health and Personal Social Services

The 1974-79 government enacted no significant legislation in the areas of health and social services policy. There had been substantial structural changes for both only shortly before Labour came to power. As far as both services were concerned, there were issues to be addressed about the distribution of resources between services and between areas. Of particular concern were the so-called 'Cinderella services' which tended to spread across the two sectors - care for various handicapped groups, in particular mentally handicapped people, and care for mentally ill people. Both Secretaries of State during this period shared the concerns of their

predecessors, Keith Joseph and Richard Crossman, about these groups. The data suggest that the 1974-79 government had some success in redistributing services in these directions. White Papers in 1976 (Department of Health and Social Security, 1976) and 1977 (Department of Health and Social Security, 1977) gave particular attention to these issues, and a planning system was developed to assist this process.

Another specialised 'preventative' health policy which secured attention in 1974 was the introduction of family planning services within the National Health Service. The Conservatives had been about to do this; the special feature of Barbara Castle's intervention on this issue was that she over-ruled her predecessor's decision that there should be charges for this service.

Throughout this book so far comparatively little attention has been paid to the personal social services. Until the 1970s they had been small in scale and their actions had seldom been politically controversial. In Chapter 5 it was suggested that the unified social services departments came into being largely because a determined professional and academic group acted effectively to get the idea past a minister, Richard Crossman, who was preoccupied by other matters. However, once established these new local authority departments were able to grow into powerful new forces in local government, second in size only to education departments. Their social problem focus and their responsibilities for services to a growing group in the population - elderly people - gave them an increasing importance. Although their growth rate was much like that of the other services over these difficult years, they secured a place for themselves in the expenditure patterns of local government that they had some success in sustaining even when local government finance came under strain in the late 1970s and early 1980s (see Webb and Wistow 1982 and 1986).

In the last chapter the new structure for the health service was described as an elaborate compromise between the different interests within the system. For Barbara Castle the doctors were to prove a particular 'handful'. Partly this had to do with the old perennial battles over doctors' pay and terms of service, but one issue (closely related to the two) assumed particular importance. It arose partly because of growing strength of unions amongst the non-professional staff of health service who saw no reason (particularly with Labour in power) why the 'syndicalism' which applied to the doctors should not to some degree apply to them too.

Labour's February 1974 manifesto included a commitment to 'phase private practice from the hospital service'. But with all the

difficulties the government faced this might have remained merely a symbolic commitment had it not been for protests from non-medical members of the National Union of Public Employees about the services supplied to a new private wing at Charing Cross Hospital in London. Clearly anger about this was fuelled by discontent over pay. The Area Health Authority's efforts to solve the problem were frustrated by British Medical Association (BMA) discontent over the solution. Barbara Castle was drawn into trying to resolve the problem, which rumbled on for some time. Eventually legislation was proposed in the Queens Speech of October 1975 to phase out pay beds. The BMA's response was to call upon all senior hospital doctors to ban all NHS work except in emergencies.

A byzantine negotiation process followed between Barbara Castle and her staff on the one side and senior officers of the BMA, plus other bodies representing the consultants, on the other. It had to deal with the shape the legislation should take, the rate at which beds should be phased out, and the circumstances under which exceptions should be allowed. There were implications, of course, for the contracts of service and pay of consultants. Much to Castle's chagrin, Harold Wilson allowed himself to be drawn in, and secured the offices of Arnold Goodman, his solicitor (who had been used for various trouble shooting tasks), as a mediator. Barbara Castle's account of all this is fascinating (Castle, 1990, intermittently between pages 655 and 758). It includes a witty account of her own misfortune in sustaining an accident during this dispute and being terrified of securing VIP treatment from a hospital for fear that it could be used in publicity against her. After laborious argument, agreement was reached on the terms for a settlement, but the negotiating doctors insisted that it should be presented to their organisations merely as a set of government proposals; some of them then deliberately urged its rejection.

Here then was medical politics at its most extreme. In the midst of all this, a Royal Commission was set up to review the future of the health service. Its terms of reference included investigating the relationship between public and private practice, but the government refused to let the Commission be used as a reason to postpone the pay beds legislation. It reported to the next Conservative government, offering a modest defence of the health service and a series of suggestions for advancing its egalitarian contribution, most of which were disregarded (Merrison Report, Cmnd.7615, 1979). By that time, too, Barbara Castle's strenuous efforts to eliminate pay beds might just as well never have taken place!

Housing

The Labour opposition had been deeply opposed to the Housing Finance Act of 1972, but it had also been embarrassed by the efforts of some local authorities, and particularly the Derbyshire District of Clay Cross, deliberately to disobey the law. Hence the government acted as quickly as possible to sweep away the earlier Act, passing, in early 1975, the Housing Rents and Subsidies Act. The only part of the 1972 Act it retained was the rebate and allowance system. The new Act gave the local authorities back their power to fix rents. It also maintained the subsidies to local authorities at the levels operating under the transitional arrangements for the implementation of the 1972 Act, and added the following:

> subsidies towards new investment costs and towards increases in the costs of servicing old debts (interest rates were rising fast at the time);

> special subsidies to help high cost areas;

> subsidies to enable rents to be kept down as part of the counter-inflationary policies of 1974-76.

Given that this was principally a return to the status quo before 1972 and that earlier subsidy arrangements had been piled on top of one another since the end of the First World War, the system was what the new Secretary of State, Anthony Crosland, described as 'a dog's breakfast. Hence he established a review.

That review was completed in 1977 when a 'consultative document' on housing policy was published (HMSO, 1977). This proposed a system that had some features in common with the Housing Finance Act but did not interfere directly with local authorities' powers to fix their own rents; nor did it necessarily entail a gradual phasing out of general purpose subsidies. The overall approach offered a potential for manipulation in a variety of ways which could be determined by the ideology of the government operating it. The system enabled central government to determine the amount of subsidy for each new year, using that of the previous year as a starting point. It could then impose its view of an appropriate level of increase in the 'local contribution' to costs, from rent and rates, using the central subsidy to make up any deficit if it thought the local authority had contributed as much as it could.

Malpass characterises this whole sequence of events in the following way:

> The period which began with the great confrontation over the Housing Finance Act ended with Labour proposing a subsidy system which was quite acceptable to the Conservatives. To the extent that there was true convergence, it was that Labour gave up opposition to deficit subsidy and the Conservatives abandoned fair rents. However... for the most part Labour... was converging on the Conservatives... (Malpass, 1990, p.132).

The Labour government fell in 1979 before it could enact this system; the Conservatives' Housing Act of 1980 essentially took it over. In determining subsidy levels in practice, the decisions of the Department of the Environment then entailed fixing 'fair rents' inasmuch as, as has been suggested earlier, that concept has any real meaning.

Education

In Labour's approximately five years in power, education was the responsibility of three different Secretaries of State: Reg Prentice (who had joined the Conservatives by 1977) from March 1974 to June 1975, Fred Mulley from June 1975 to September 1976 and Shirley Williams (later to be a founder member of the SDP) for the rest of Labour's period of office. Earlier in this book it was suggested that education policy has tended to be very civil service dominated. It might be concluded therefore that there is nothing more to say about the politics of education policy over this period. In fact there were two important and to some extent contradictory events deserving attention.

One was that, after the battles over using 'government by circular' to try to get local authorities to develop comprehensive secondary education systems from 1964 to 1970, the government now decided to legislate. The 1976 Education Act gave the Secretary of State powers to compel local authorities, who had not done so, to submit proposals for comprehensive reorganisation. By 1981 (a date a couple of years into the period of Conservative rule has been chosen because of the time this change process takes), about 83 per cent of children in state education in England, and 96 per cent in Scotland and Wales, were in comprehensive schools. The contrasting figures for 1975 were 64 per cent and 87 per cent.

The other event was the launching of what was described as the 'great debate' on education. In 1976 James Callaghan made a speech at Oxford in which he argued that the education system should give more attention to providing education relevant to the needs of industry. He made particular comments about engineering but also suggested that there might be some more general problems about the extent to which children were being equipped with basic skills. The Department of Education then launched a series of regional conferences and published a document on the need for a core curriculum. These events occurred at a time when unemployment was starting to rise again, the natural consequence of the deflationary policies of the time, and youth unemployment was appearing as a prominent component of that rise. All this, coming from the party which had championed comprehensive education, was most welcome to the educationalists who had been involved in the Black Paper ventures (Cox and Dyson, 1969a, 1969b, 1970; Cox and Boyson, 1975, 1977). It may be suggested that Callaghan was here trying to pre-empt the Conservatives on this issue. The 'great debate' was to be taken much further and to have a fundamental impact on policy in the 1980s.

Conclusions

There is no easy way to sum up the social policy of the 1974-79 Labour governments. There is a temptation to analyse it in terms of pre-IMF and post-IMF events, or to distinguish between the Wilson and the Callaghan regimes. It is important to highlight (even though she has done this very well for herself) the special way in which the efforts of one determined minister, Barbara Castle, whose front-line participation ended with Wilson's, shone through as a contribution to the advancement of social policy. It is important to recognise that the Labour party became deeply divided, in a way which undermined its challenge to Thatcherism in the 1980s, between those (some of whom formed the Social Democratic Party) who saw no option but to cut back the role of the state and those who strove to find ways to protect the party's socialist ideals within which defence of the welfare state figured so prominently.

But why just focus upon the Labour party? This chapter and the previous one must be considered together. Whilst Labour have, since 1945, been seen as the champions of the welfare state it has nevertheless been argued earlier in the book that the Conservatives shared, albeit in a muted and sometimes divided form, a commitment to welfare. The whole period 1970 to 1979 may be seen, therefore, as one in which the increasingly strong manifestations of Britain's economic problems - inflation and unemployment increasing together, the falling value of the pound on the foreign exchanges and industrial conflict - forced everyone to re-appraise the spending programmes of the state, in which welfare, as much for demographic reasons as for any other, figured so significantly. The two chapters have sought to tease out some of the contradictions in the resultant search behaviour, contradictions which were bound to be particularly manifest on the Labour side because of its more egalitarian and more statist ideology.

Finally, the other important point about this chapter is that what it has to say should be considered very carefully before proceeding to look at the Thatcher era. It has become all too easy for those who are hostile to the emergent ideology to fall into the trap of believing that in 1979 a wicked witch emerged to cast a spell over the British welfare state. That view is embodied in the fact that 'ism' has been so readily added to the end of Thatcher's name. It will be the task of the next chapter to show that the situation was not as simple as that.

This is certainly the view of the person who, as Labour Chancellor of the Exchequer, presided over the public sector cuts of the 1974-79 period. Denis Healey, in his autobiography, pungently argues:

> Mrs Thatcher did not create what is now called Thatcherism out of the blue. She gave expression to feelings which were already colouring public opinion on both sides of the Atlantic.....
>
> The Labour Party in Britain, like the liberal Democrats in the United States, for a long time refused to recognise this secular shift in public opinion. When at last they found it impossible to ignore, they would not admit how far it was justified, partly because it was nourished by their own shortcomings both in government and opposition. So while the Labour Parties in Australia and New Zealand, and the Socialist Parties in France, Italy and Spain came to terms with the new political mood - and won electoral support by doing so - the British Labour Party allowed Mrs Thatcher to monopolise the opportunities it presented (Healey, 1989, p.486).

This highlights some of the contradictions in Britain's politics over this period. It was Labour which had to respond to the 'oil shock', before Britain was really established as an oil producer, and to cut public expenditure in response to IMF pressure in 1976. Having reacted (some would say 'over-reacted') to this crisis, the government appeared to be bringing both unemployment and inflation under control when its always turbulent accord with the trade unions fell apart in the 'winter of discontent' in 1978-79.

It has been the task of this chapter especially, but also of the previous one and in some respects the whole book, to make it clear how difficult it has been for those who tried to protect and advance welfare ideals; and to show how equivocal and complex government support for the welfare state has been, regardless of the ostensible ideology of those in power.

8   Thatcher's Conservative Governments 1979-90

Introduction

There were three general elections between 1979 and 1990, only the first of which produced a change of party control. After 1979 perhaps the most dramatic political event was the dethronement of Margaret Thatcher by her own party in November 1990. As pointed out in the introduction this event has been chosen as the end point for this chapter and for this book as a whole, rather than the general election in April 1992, at which John Major secured another electoral mandate for the Conservative Party whose leadership he took over. However, in various places and particularly at the end of the present chapter, there will be some observations on post-Thatcher Conservatism.

Margaret Thatcher replaced Edward Heath as Conservative leader in 1975. Under her leadership the party gradually began to put together both a programme and a statement of Conservative philosophy, which would mark it out as different from the party which had governed under Heath. Keith Joseph was the key ideologue, fiercely endorsing free market views and turning his back on the sort of paternalistic Toryism which had characterised his earlier ministerial career (Halcrow, 1989). The new approach was initially more evident in statements on economic and industrial policy rather than in what was said about social policy. There were some specific pledges: on the sale of council houses, on ceasing to force local authorities to make all their secondary schools comprehensive and on stopping the phasing out of pay beds in hospitals. But much was vague in the Conservatives' plans. The main threat to social policy lay in economic policies which would cut public expenditure. The government was committed to cutting expenditure overall, but to increasing it on defence and law and order and to keeping it level on the health service. The object of this cutting was to make possible cuts in taxation.

When first elected leader, Margaret Thatcher was not particularly effective as either a Parliamentary or a public performer. Despite the Labour government's difficulties, the Conservatives did not move sharply ahead in the opinion polls. Callaghan rejected the idea, advocated by many of his colleagues, of calling an election in Autumn 1978. During the following months Labour's efforts at pay control systematically fell apart in a series of acrimonious disputes. Legislation offering a measure of devolution, designed more to try to keep nationalist party support for Labour than to effect convincing constitutional change, ran into difficulties when a referendum produced a rejection of the measure in Wales and only a narrow majority in support in Scotland. Labour lost a motion of 'no confidence' in its rule in the House of Commons on 28 March 1979. Callaghan dissolved Parliament and a general election was held on 3 May.

The Conservatives won about 44 per cent of the vote and 339 seats. Labour obtained 37 per cent of the vote and only 269 seats. The Liberals obtained 11 seats and the other, mainly Irish, parties 16. The Conservatives strengthened their position in 1983, gaining 397 seats despite a fall in their proportion of the vote to about 42 per cent. In 1987 a similar proportion of the vote yielded 376 seats (variations in results during this period depending very much upon the variations in the relative strengths of the disorganised Labour Party and the Liberal/SDP Alliance). The Conservatives won again, fairly narrowly under Major in 1992.

A distinctively Thatcherite social policy emerged slowly. In attempting to characterise it the obvious starting point is to look at social expenditure as a whole. When this is done data are found which do not seem to fit with either the portrait of Thatcherism propagated by its opponents or the impression that Margaret Thatcher herself often set out to create.

In earlier chapters it has been shown that growth rates for social expenditure were around 5 per cent per annum between 1964 and 1975. They then dropped sharply. Whilst the data in Table 8.1, roughly comparing the period of Labour rule with Thatcher's era, suggest a slight 'Thatcher effect' upon social expenditure, if the initial period of high spending by Labour were eliminated from the first column, that effect would entirely disappear. In many respects Denis Healey was a more effective 'butcher' of public expenditure than Margaret Thatcher's Chancellors.

An alternative way of analysing public expenditure is in terms of its relationship to the Gross Domestic Product. In 1970 it was just over 40 per cent of GDP. In 1975 it peaked at almost 50 per cent. It was brought down to about 43 per cent in 1979. Then it rose again a couple of percentage points in the early 1980s before dropping away to 40 per cent in 1990. However the problem with this statistic is that it is more strongly influenced by the health of the economy than by trends in public expenditure. When the figures for 1992 come to be produced they will show that a combination of an pre-election boom in expenditure with a severe recession will yield one of the highest peace-time percentages ever. In the light of the 1979 commitment to cutting expenditure overall, but to increasing it on defence and law and order and protecting the health service, 'disproportionate cut-backs in other programmes were required' (Thain and Wright, 1990, p.6). Thain and Wright go on to show that in order to try to maintain some credibility for their commitment to cuts, the Thatcher governments sought alternative ways to define public expenditure and treated receipts from privatisation sales as 'negative expenditure' as opposed to showing them in income accounts. Despite these measures they were forced to change their target first to the avoidance of an increase in expenditure and later to a quest to secure the reduction of public expenditure as a proportion of the Gross Domestic Product. Finally, by the end of the decade even the commitments on defence and law and order had to be revised in the face of the other upward pressures on expenditure.

Table 8.1   *Public expenditure percentage growth per annum 1973-91 (in real terms)*

	1973-74 to 1978-79	1978-79 to 1990-91
Social security	5.4	3.0
Health and personal social services	2.0	3.4
Education	0	1.3
Housing	3.0	-4.8
All expenditure	1.8	1.1

Sources: Central Statistical Office, *Social Trends* and *National Income and Expenditure*, annual publications.

Table 8.1 provides data relating to above discussion, together with figures on individual expenditure programmes. Government accounting procedures have not been consistent over time. Overall figures depend upon changing accounting conventions, while individual budget figures may be affected by changes in policy and in administrative structure. A particularly important example of the latter concerns the housing figures where a shift of policy on subsidies to low-income tenants moved a significant block of expenditure from the housing to the social security accounts during the 1980s. Recent work by Hills and his colleagues corrects for some of these problems (Hills, 1990) but has not been used here because it does not cover the whole period under discussion. Their work points to broadly similar conclusions but indicates that these figures exaggerate the decline in housing expenditure.

There has been a considerable debate in Britain about health expenditure trends. While Thatcher used data like that set out above to claim that the health service remained safe under her rule, her critics suggested that standards of service had fallen. To evaluate this argument there is a need to bear in mind certain factors which can lead to an increase in health service costs without any actual service improvement. There are two aspects to this, one which can be described as concerning 'needs'. Thus, official estimates have been made that health service expenditure needs to rise by at least 2 per cent per annum to keep pace with the increasing numbers of elderly people and with improvements in medical technology. Some commentators have suggested that this figure is too low (Robinson and Judge, 1988). The other issue concerns 'resources'. The costs of inputs of actual care resources may rise, pushing up overall costs but not output. It is necessary to try to take into account ways in which care delivery costs have inflated faster than the general rate of inflation (the 'relative price effect' problem, see Heald, 1983, pp.114-18 and 177-86). Two potential issues here are drug costs and staff costs. As far as the latter are concerned pay increases, even when they are only marginally above the inflation rate, may have a substantial impact in a labour-intensive service like health.

The study by Hills and his colleagues included some work on this problem which reached a conclusion reverses the contrast between the Labour and Conservative regimes suggested by table 8.1:

> Both governments increased the overall volume of *resources* going to the NHS. However, the annual growth rate in resources was higher under Labour than under the Conservatives - according to one measure, over four times as high - while the growth in *need* (or demand) was higher under the Conservatives than under Labour. Hence the increase in resources relative to need was substantially greater under Labour than under the Conservatives (Hills et al. 1990, pp.131-2).

The only difficulty with this argument, which is supported by some careful analysis, is that there was a significant growth in health expenditure at the end of the 1980s, in the run-up period to the 1992 election, outside the period analysed by Hills and his colleagues. However, the ups and downs of this 'electoral business cycle' bedevil public expenditure analysis; at the time of writing, a post-election public expenditure downturn is being confidently forecast.

A similar kind of analysis needs to be applied to education expenditure, although in this case the demographic effect is broadly downwards. In education policy there are rather safer grounds for arguing that growth rates in the Thatcher era seem to have been higher than in the period of Labour rule in the late 1970s. It is relevant to note here Le Grand's argument that health and education policy expenditures do not have egalitarian effects (Le Grand, 1982), and his subsequent work which identifies these amongst the issues where middle-class interests protect social policy (Goodin and Le Grand, eds., 1987).

This last point is particularly relevant when attention is turned to the other two areas of social policy highlighted above - social security and housing - where expenditure growth was much less (in fact negative in the case of housing) in the period of Margaret Thatcher's rule. In the case of housing, what nearly disappeared during this era was central subsidy of public sector housing, except through means-tested benefits (shown above in the social security accounts). Subsidy of mortgage interest, a housing 'benefit' for the better off, does not show as public expenditure at all; it is seen as tax income foregone.

Despite the transfer of some of the housing subsidy costs to social security and, more importantly, despite the fact that an ageing population builds an automatic cost escalator into social security costs (in the same way as into health service costs) the growth rate of social security expenditure was lower in the 1980s than in the last period of Labour rule. Something else which makes this remarkable is that the higher unemployment of the 1980s was also a considerable source of pressure on the social security budget. What we can deduce from this is that the Thatcher governments made strenuous efforts to curb social security costs. Evidence from legislative activity to confirm that statement is considerable. The following measures can be identified:

- Changes to the uprating rules - in the 1970s the rule determining inflation-proofing for the levels of many benefits was that they should go up with either earnings or prices, whichever was higher. The Conservatives changed the general rules to take only prices into account and on some occasions deliberately refused to uprate some benefits at all (child benefit particularly suffered from this).

- Cuts to insurance benefits - abolition of earnings-related supplements to short-term benefits; replacement of sickness benefit by statutory sick pay; tightening of qualifying rules for unemployment benefit; abolition of maternity and death grants.

- Cutting of means-tested benefits by 'simplification'; the steepening of the rates at which they taper off as individual incomes rise; the abolition of entitlements to special additional grants.

- Efforts to prevent certain groups from getting entitlements at all - youngsters aged under 18; full-time students; married female labour market participants; prematurely retired people with private pensions.

- The operation of more rigorous controls to prevent claims from unemployed people not 'actively seeking work'; to increase contributions from 'responsible' males to unsupported mothers; to prevent fraudulent claims.

The complexity of these cutback measures makes it difficult to quantify them as a whole. Some relevant contextual points can however be made. The official unemployment rate rose from an annual average around 3 per cent in 1974, through about 5 per cent in 1979 to peak at above 12 per cent in 1983, then dipped a little but came back to around 8-9 per cent by the early 1990s (figures based on OECD estimates). These high levels were reported despite strenuous efforts to revise the statistics so that significant numbers of unemployed were no longer counted (see McCarthy, ed., 1989, p.137). There seems little doubt that unemployment, accompanied also by Conservative legislation to weaken the power of the trade unions, has had a significant effect upon wage levels. At the bottom end of the income distribution the government has undermined policies designed to prevent very low wages. Significantly, such employment growth occurred in the late 1980s was concentrated amongst low-pay sectors - service industries, part-time female work and very insecure forms of self-employment. All of these facts will have tended to increase the underlying need for benefits, both to support people without work and to subsidise low-income work. In the absence of the countervailing cuts, they would have pushed up social security expenditure sharply.

As suggested in various ways earlier in this book, the notion of a 'crisis' about welfare expenditure has been present since the mid-1970s. But Margaret Thatcher addressed the task of dealing with the so-called crisis with very much more enthusiasm than her predecessors. What has characterised Thatcherism has moreover not merely been the readiness to proclaim an ideological mission, but also an acceptance of this as an anti-egalitarian one in which little concern has been shown for the victims of cuts or of rising unemployment. The welfare cuts and the combination of tax cutting with severe public expenditure restraints have been justified in terms of the need to set entrepreneurs free and eliminate the 'nanny state'. The doctrine that growth will come if individuals are free to enrich themselves and that thus 'a rising tide will lift all the boats' has been enunciated by those who feel they need to justify 'soaking the rich' (Joseph and Sumption, 1979).

In Chapters 3 and 4 of this book there were brief mentions of trends in income tax rates. After that period any systematic analysis of taxation trends requires a complex analysis beyond the remit of this book. Trends in basic rates need to be related to trends in other rates, both above and below them. Then together they need to be related to rules about tax exemptions and tax thresholds. These affect the levels of income at which individuals come into the tax net or incur higher rates of tax, and the kinds of income which are exempted from tax. Finally, income tax is by no means the only tax; there are therefore issues about its role relative to other taxes as a source of government revenue. In relation to all of this complicated subject it is, however, important to recognise that the 1980s was a decade when the government systematically lightened income tax for higher income tax-payers and shifted the tax burden from direct to indirect taxation (a measure in itself generally regressive).

Thatcherism is not merely economic liberalism. The title of a recent book *The Free Economy and the Strong State* (Gamble, 1988) perhaps best captures the essence of Thatcherism. The strong state has been seen as necessary for reasons going beyond the mission to curb trade unions and the need to cope with the law and order problems of a 'free economy'. In addition the central state has tried to use social policies to reassert a traditional definition of the family. Far from being opponents of 'social engineering', modern Conservative ideologues have seemed to relish the opportunity to try to use social policy to change behaviour. In doing this they have explored new approaches under the influence of various New Right thinkers, including people like Charles Murray (1984) from the United States whose 'lessons' for social policy derive from the examination of a very differently organised welfare system.

There are particular manifestations of both of these ideological currents in Thatcherite social security policy; the next section will give this some attention, focusing particularly upon the events starting with the enactment of many of the ideas considered in the Supplementary Benefit review (see last chapter) through the introduction of housing benefit and the establishment of statutory sick pay to the Fowler reviews of social security which produced the 1986 Social Security Act.

Another thread in the policies of the Thatcher government has been a commitment to privatisation. This is difficult to analyse because of the multiple forms of that phenomenon as well as the multiple motives likely to be involved (see discussion in Ascher, 1987). The Thatcher governments can be seen as going through three phases of privatisation. First, immediately on coming to power they forced local authorities to sell houses to their tenants, often at large discounts. In this phase the other key thrust of privatisation was towards reducing trade union power. Efforts were made to develop ways of putting hitherto public sector work - services like cleaning, catering, building maintenance and transport which were operated as part of the health service or local government etc. - into the hands of private contractors, who had to tender competitively for the work.

The second phase was dominated by sales of major public utilities - the telephone system, gas, electricity and water. This had many social effects, particularly inasmuch as the prices for these necessary services were pushed up, but these may generally be regarded as outside the concerns of this book.

In the third phase the government's privatisation ambitions have widened. Kites were flown about radically transforming health and education services, through the introduction of charges and voucher systems; but the changes adopted consisted of facilitating the development of semi-autonomous publicly funded units within the public sector. For instance, in its community care initiative (HMSO, Cm. 849, 1989), the aim is to encourage private residential homes and private home care organisations to tender for public contracts. In all the caring services, internal management arrangements are being developed which involve service 'purchasers' making contracts with service 'providers'. The latter may be separate parts of the purchasing organisation, separate public bodies, voluntary non-profit-making organisations or private profit-oriented bodies.

Thus privatisation, interpreted widely and loosely, provides three case studies for this chapter. One section will look at the sale of council houses to their occupiers and at efforts in the 1988 Housing Act to sell them to new landlords too.

The next case study looks at some of the ways in which the privatisation ideology has led to the creation of publicly accountable and publicly funded semi-autonomous agencies and organisations. These may be just new ways of organising public services, but many regard them as first steps towards privatisation.

The final case study related to the privatisation theme will look at community care, where a complex policy process is occurring in which privatisation issues, social security issues and issues about the role of local government are mixed up together.

This leads logically on to a section which concerns the ways in which central-local government relations and local taxation have been changed, with considerable implications for many aspects of social policy.

Finally themes about privatisation and about central-local relations will arise again in a final case study section on education, exploring where the 'great debate' initiated by James Callaghan in the 1970s (see the last chapter) has led to in the 1980s.

Social Security: The Erosion of the Beveridge Principles

The pressure groups, who had experienced extensive consultation under Labour, urging the government to honour the party's commitment to Child Benefit and participating in the Supplementary Benefit review, found themselves shut out by the new government. It's first steps were to move quickly to act upon most of the recommendations of the Supplementary Benefits review, apart from the lump sum payment idea (Walker, 1983). It also introduced a housing benefit scheme, pushing together in an untidy way rent rebates and allowances and the Supplementary Benefit provisions for the support of rent.

The government reduced the value of contributory benefits by altering the procedure for inflation-related increases, and by extending the taxation of benefits. It shifted responsibility for the provision of sickness absence for the first 28 weeks from the national insurance scheme to a statutory sick pay scheme to be run by employers.

Having moved so quickly to make the above changes to the benefit schemes, the government soon found it had further anomalies to deal with. To many people's surprise, the more rule based Supplementary Benefit scheme was more open to applications for special payments for extra help than the old discretionary scheme had been, despite the virtual abolition of clothing grants (Berthoud, 1985). If the pressure groups could do little to influence policy directly, they at least found some ways to act effectively as the advocates of individuals who were seeking benefits. The government was disconcerted by the rapid rise of single payments. On top of this, the new housing benefit proved inefficient in operation (Kemp and Raynsford, eds., 1984).

In 1983 the Secretary of State, Norman Fowler, decided that a more radical reform of social security was necessary. As explained above, social security was an element in public expenditure which the government was finding very hard to control. Proclaiming himself to be engaged in the most radical review of social security since Beveridge, Fowler set up a number of ministerially dominated committees to explore options for reform.

The outcome was a report, published in 1985 (Secretary of State for Social Services, Cmnd. 9517, 1985) which declared that the social security system had 'lost its way'. It identified a need for better targeting of benefits and simpler systems, in themselves uncontroversial aspirations, but it set these in a context of a need for economy which was bound to make them difficult to achieve.

As well as proposing simplified mean-tested benefits, the report set out the view that the State Earnings Pension Scheme (SERPS) would impose excessive burdens on future generations. Fowler's initial idea was to replace the latter altogether by a funded scheme, but then he drew back when he recognised what heavy short-term costs the government would impose upon itself inasmuch as it lost the use of contributions to fund current benefits. In the end, instead he weakened the benefits guaranteed under SERPS to the detriment of shorter-term contributors such as married women, relaxed the conditions for alternative private schemes and adopted measures to encourage new kinds of private 'personal pensions'. When all the records of this decision- making process are available, it may well prove fruitful to investigate why the government were so concerned about pensions costs which would not fall on the Exchequer until far into the future, to the extent that it was initially prepared to reduce current income. It may well be found that a desire to benefit the private pensions industry lay at the root of this measure.

The 1986 Social Security Act modified SERPS (in the way outlined above), replaced Supplementary Benefit by Income Support, and Family Income Supplement by Family Credit. These two new schemes were given simpler rule structures than that of Supplementary Benefit. Housing benefit was also altered to bring it in line with these other two benefits. The government proclaimed that it was effectively attacking the 'poverty trap' (see discussion in Chapter 6) by these measures. In fact it replaced the poverty trap's rather haphazard operation, based upon different rules tending to operate at different times and with bizarre effects which exceptionally created a reduction of income, with a system which made the 'super tax' effect higher for most people, rising to 98 per cent for some taxpayers who were recipients of both Family Credit and housing benefit. A desire to prevent housing support for rent payers extending a long way up the income distribution, as housing policy moved steadily towards a structure of market-level rents, was influential in producing the very sharp 'taper' which exacerbated the poverty trap (perhaps now better described,as in Deacon and Bradshaw, 1983, as a 'poverty plateau').

The maternity grant and the death grant, two benefits initiated in the Beveridge era but then, over the years, not properly updated in line with inflation, were abolished, to be replaced by means-test related benefits for the very poor. But the change to single payments which attracted a great deal of attention was the replacement of entitlements to these payments, available under the Supplementary Benefit scheme to help people with specific needs, by a much more limited system, known as the Social Fund. Under this new scheme 70 per cent of expenditure was to be in the form of loans, and budgets were to be strictly 'cash-limited. There was a major protest, and many social workers resolved to try to make the scheme difficult to operate. This resistance proved ineffectual. The use of advocacy to try to maximise the help poor people received from means tests was severely restricted by this measure. The government had found a way to 'trump' the welfare rights movement and prevent it undermining economy objectives in the way it had with the earlier changes.

Rising unemployment, as the government used monetary policy to curb inflation, pushed up social security costs. In response the benefits designed to protect the unemployed were substantially weakened. 'Simplification' reduced the help available to all young people; later measures made support for under 18s conditional upon undergoing training. Penalties for anyone refusing to go on training schemes and for leaving jobs were made much more severe.

Some of its critics saw it the measured implemented as a result of the Fowler review as contributing to the destruction of the Beveridge scheme (Lister, 1986). Clearly the review was influenced by a concern with 'targeting' which saw insurance-type entitlements as too open ended. Clearly also the development of simpler means tests, operating in comparative harmony with each other (compared with what went before), was influenced by a view that negative income tax represented an appropriate way forward for British social security. Means-tested benefits were clearly put near the centre of the system. However, an overall assessment of this measure needs to examine at the combined impact of both the Thatcher and the Heath governments' changes to social security and to put them in the context of the changes in British society and its economy since Beveridge (see Parker, 1989; Hill, 1990). This will be done in a section in the final chapter which will examine the role the debate between universalism and selectivity has played in the politics of British social policy.

Selling Council Houses

The Conservative party had advocated the selling of council houses to their occupiers for some years. While the Labour party generally, and some Labour local authorities in particular, resisted this policy, their stance on this issue had begun to become modified by the 1970s.

In 1979 the Conservatives included a commitment in their election manifesto to provide a statutory 'right' for council tenants to buy the houses they were renting. The Housing Act of 1980 provides that right to buy - at market prices less a discount based on length of tenancy. Later legislation extended these provisions. Such a 'right' can obviously only be exercised if an individual has resources. When the legislation was first passed, the process of establishing a capacity to buy and securing a valuation seemed to set up some barriers which might be exploited by local authorities eager to restrict its implementation. In practice the government very effectively put pressure on those Labour-controlled authorities which tried to do this, going so far in one case, Norwich, as to secure legal intervention to enable it to put in a special commissioner to do the job (Forrest and Murie, 1988, Chapter 9).

Social Trends describes the impact of this policy as follows:

> As a result of this legislation, almost 1.5 million local authority and new town tenants bought their homes during the 1980s. Annual sales peaked at 226 thousand in 1982, but fell to less than half this level in 1985 and 1986. Between 1986 and 1989 sales increased in each year before falling again in 1990 when only 140 thousand dwellings were sold... (*Social Trends* 22, 1992, p.147).

The Labour party was placed in a difficult position in opposing this measure. By the 1980s owner-occupation had so clearly become the preferred housing tenure for all who could afford it. The Secretary of State, Michael Heseltine, skilfully presented himself, in introducing the measure, as liberating ordinary people from the 'barons' who controlled vast bureaucratic local government housing empires. Whilst the ugly tower blocks where many of the poorest local authority tenants lived were not much affected by the 'right to buy' policy, they did little good for the image of public housing. The tenants who bought, often in the nicer quality low-rise and green council estates, were able to change their homes, by minor additions, into more individual looking 'Englishmen's castles'. They thus often enhanced their prospects of geographical mobility or of the sort of capital gain secured by many owner-occupiers in the property boom of the mid-1980s and had an asset to pass on to survivors. It has been suggested that this measure did a great deal to enhance support for the Conservative party amongst manual workers in the south of England. Whilst the evidence from electoral studies is ambiguous (see discussion in Forrest and Murie, 1988, 100-106) this is certainly a conclusion which the Labour party has drawn.

Criticisms of the policy rested upon the extent to which it weakened the capacity of local authorities to respond to housing need. This was reinforced by government-imposed rules which prevented the ploughing back of all the receipts from sales into new housing investment. The combination of this with very low levels of investment in public housing contributed to increases in levels of homelessness.

An even more complicated criticism, out of which it would be hard for opposition parties to make political capital, is that the sale of 'good' houses to better off tenants has enhanced social polarisation in housing (Forrest and Murie, 1988). The longstanding problem for cities of a gap between the 'good' estates and the 'bad' has been exacerbated. The measure reinforces the tendency for public sector housing to be housing for the poor. By 1986-87 almost two-thirds of local authority tenants were on means-tested benefits (figure from a Parliamentary answer quoted by Forrest and Murie, op.cit. p.69).

The tendency for all who could buy to do so and for those left behind to be dependant on benefits is being further reinforced by policies which push rent levels up, leaving subsidy to the benefit system.

The 1988 Housing Act added a new approach to the sale of council houses. It set up what the government misleadingly called a 'pick a landlord' scheme to encourage the transfer of the control over local authority housing to new types of approved social landlords. In its implementation it was, of course, the landlords that had to do the picking, by making offers for areas or blocks of local authority houses; or alternatively, local authorities who had to seek housing associations to which they might transfer their stock. There were weak safeguards for tenants, involving a peculiar voting arrangement for groups likely to be affected which made it difficult to secure a veto. This new development depended a great deal upon its implementation (a theme which will arise increasingly in the rest of this chapter). In fact it initially did little to change the shape of public housing. It involved housing associations as the new social landlords rather than outright private entrepreneurs. A limited number of local authorities, mainly in Southern England, transferred their stock in this way. At the time of writing there are further developments on this theme.

New Institutions for Policy Delivery in the Health Service and Elsewhere

An important feature of the social policy of the Thatcher governments (and beyond) has been the breaking up of many of the big state bureaucracies to create organisations for the implementation of policy separate from the central policy-making ministries. In some cases, particularly in the health service, this has been taken further to offer the possibility of a selection of operational agencies which may to some degree be in competition and may offer the citizen some measure of choice. It is too early to judge how realisable these last two possibilities are. These developments have not included extending local government's role as a service provider, for reasons which will be explored further below.

These developments may be interpreted in various ways:

(1) As largely symbolic ways of seeming to roll back the state, extend choice or increase open government whilst not really doing so.

(2) As ways of liberating middle and lower ranking public servants to act innovatively outside a stultifying bureaucracy.

(3) As the creation of forms of internal competition - quasi-markets - which extend choice and/or enhance efficiency.

(4) As the first steps towards real privatisation which will bring social services under private sector management and control.

(5) As the first steps towards privatisation which will not only mean private control but also that social services (for long supplied free or heavily subsidised by the state) will actually have to be purchased on an open market.

The extreme Right hope that they are going right through to the fifth alternative; the Left suspects that this is the ultimate objective of the government. The ideological context often makes it difficult to judge dispassionately measures which are presented in terms of categories (2) and (3). It may be pointed out that social democratic regimes like Sweden have accepted the division between policy-making and implementing agencies for a long while. It may be shown, for example, that the new social security agencies are working harder than the old department ever did to try to be approachable and to make their offices less unpleasant places. However, as suggested above, these new approaches to implementation may unleash forces for change which will subsequently be hard to bring back under the sorts of controls associated with the earlier concept of a welfare state. In that earlier concept, central accountability and central planning (however inexpertly practised) were deemed to be important to attack territorial and class-related inequalities and to ensure universal access. These may be under threat, the writings of the Conservative ideologues certainly reinforce that suspicion.

Clearly much more could be said about these developments, which affect every area of social policy, than is possible here. This section will be concluded instead with some brief comments on developments in the health service (though the issue will surface briefly again in later sections on community care and on education). Health is a particularly important testing ground for the arguments rehearsed above because much of the drive for change in the National Health Service came (a) from rising political concerns about cost control and (b) from arguments within Conservative ranks that privatisation should be pursued. Recognition of the NHS's continuing popularity with the electorate, restrained the government from following the outright privatisation ideas very far. However, it looked across the Atlantic (despite the fact that actual health expenditure there - when private and public outgoings are combined - is vast by British standards) for ideas on how to develop what have come to be known as 'internal market' systems. One particular American expert made a lightening tour of Britain and set out his ideas in a pamphlet short enough to be read by politicians (Enthoven, 1985).

Before this the Thatcher government had already made one attempt to simplify the byzantine structure set up by Sir Keith Joseph (now a leading Right Wing ideologist) by adopting measures recommended by a businessman, Roy Griffiths (Department of Health and Social Security, 1983). After a further enquiry, whose conclusions were set out in a series of glossy booklets, it legislated in 1990.

This legislation, which streamlined the main control structure, also allowed for the setting up of National Health Service Trusts. These are semi-autonomous bodies, ultimately answerable to the Secretary of State which are able to manage their own finances, appoint their own staff and plan a package of services which they 'sell' to the District Health Authorities. The latter are required to act as purchasers of services on behalf of the patients in their area. They may make those purchases from the units (hospital groups etc.) under their direct control, from units in other Districts or from Trusts.

The new Trusts may also engage in private work. Most of the Trusts are hospitals or groups of hospitals, but in some cases community units and ambulance services have become trusts. There is a steady growth of Trusts. This is beginning to become a 'stampede' as units fear they may become disadvantaged if they do not follow the trend.

In addition, general medical practitioners are allowed to apply to become 'fund holders' able to make independent arrangements with hospital providers for the needs of their own patients. This development is occurring more slowly since complicated financial management arrangements are needed within each practice to enable it to proceed.

For the analyst of social policy it is interesting to observe the complex process by which policy change is being led by institutional change. Since, as accounts earlier in this book have shown, battles between governments and the medical profession have been a central part of the politics of the NHS, there is now the possibility that governments will find it easier to rule a divided and quasi competitive system. Doctors may find it less easy take united action against the government. Trade unions are likely to find it difficult to protect wage levels across the board since individual trusts can impose their own terms of service. On the other hand, American experience suggests that even in a privately dominated health system it is hard to develop genuine competitive forces which might lower medical costs (and rewards). However, while an academic industry is getting going to try to test the arguments between traditional bureaucratic control methods and quasi-markets and to try to sort out what the latter really means (Le Grand, 1990; Harrison and Wistow, 1992; Hudson, 1992), concerns are being raised about the longer run implications of these developments for the availability of free health services.

Community and Institutional Care

It has been pointed out more than once that an ageing population has increased the pressure upon both social security and health expenditure, fuelling the search (in the light of the belief that public expenditure must be kept under tight control) for new approaches to social policy. That same issue comes up in a particularly acute form in the area of social care policy, which is - of course - principally the responsibility of the local authority social services departments. The need for care for elderly people is a public issue for a variety of reasons. Demographic change and geographical mobility have sharply reduced the availability of care within the family. There is also argument about the extent to which the extended family should be held responsible, particularly as the burden of this falls disproportionately on female relatives (Finch and Groves, 1983; Land and Rose, 1985). The private purchase of care is a feasible option for only a minority of the elderly, though most can make some contribution to this cost, even if only through the use of their social security benefits.

Hence, whilst an enormous proportion of the care of elderly people is still in the hands of relatives or friends, there is a growing need for publicly provided or subsidised care. That may be provided within an institution, within sheltered housing or through services within the home.

Before proceeding further, a semantic confusion needs to be addressed. All the forms of social care described above tend to be called, in Britain, community care, even though some of it is provided in institutions. It seems that this expression has arisen because of the distinction between this 'social' care and hospital care.

Local authority social services departments have had the responsibility to provide all these forms of 'social care', and they obviously have incentives to provide whichever forms are cheapest. However, there are some complicated boundary problems between the health service and the social services departments and between social services and housing departments. Authorities will tend to shift costs on to other agencies when they can.

The solution of some of these boundary problems has been further complicated by the existence of a private care sector which has been partly supported by public funds through the income maintenance system. Private care homes obviously reduce the burden upon statutory care providers. They have made it easier for local authorities to maintain an adequate supply of residential places. But their existence has also created distortions in attempts to plan residential care provisions and has, in a sense, 'frustrated' the move towards cheaper forms of community care by providing new residential resources some of which are used for people deemed not to be in need of such care (Audit Commission, 1986). Individuals in private residential care have been able to apply for

Supplementary Benefit (or, after the 1986 Act, Income Support). Their benefit level was determined by the amount by which the charge for residential care, plus a small 'personal' cash allowance, exceeded their other income resources. Many low-income elderly people thus obtained state help to pay for private residential care. The Department of Social Security did not always meet these charges in full; relatives were often called upon to 'top them up'.

Before 1980 the Department of Health and Social Security kept a tight limit on the charges it would meet. Then the rules were relaxed and local social security office managers were given considerable discretion to accept higher charges. Thus the Conservative Secretary of State was placed in a dilemma between his commitment to the development of the private sector and his concern to keep income maintenance expenditure under control. Then, in 1983, he imposed national limits. These were nevertheless much higher than had prevailed before 1980 when commercial home charges were rarely met. There followed a dramatic growth of private sector homes.

A report on community care by the 'watchdog' body set up by the government to undertake monitoring and 'value for money' studies on local expenditure - the Audit Commission - talked of the 'perverse effects of social security policies' in this area of care. It pointed out that anyone entitled to means-tested benefit 'who chose to live in a residential home is entitled to allowances' up to the limit imposed by the benefit rules. It went on:

> In short, the more residential the care, the easier it is to obtain benefits, and the greater the size of payment. And Supplementary Benefit funding cannot be targeted towards those individuals most in need of residential care. Nor are homes judged on whether they are giving value for money within the category of care for which they are registered (Audit Commission, 1986, p.44).

The Audit Commission team was very concerned about the extent to which this income maintenance subsidy of residential care distorted the pattern of care in the country as a whole. It noted the extent to which private homes are unevenly distributed geographically, commenting on their high incidence in the relatively prosperous southern and south-western parts of England. The consequences of this was, it said, that 'while central government attempts to achieve equitable distribution of public funds across the country, through the use of complex formulae within the National Health Service and local government, the effects can be largely offset by Supplementary Benefit payments for board and lodging' (ibid., p.3).

After the Audit Commission report on community care, the government commissioned Sir Roy Griffiths to make recommendations on community care policies as a whole. His recommendations were set out in the second influential report associated with his name (Griffiths, 1988; the other - mentioned above - dealt with the organisation of the NHS). Griffiths suggested that there should be a system under which local authority social services departments decided on social, not income, grounds that care was necessary and then had a responsibility to ensure that individuals obtained that care, either from the public or private sector. If individuals were unable to pay the care costs from the standard social security benefits or from other income, it would then be the responsibility of the local authority to provide a subsidy.

The government accepted these recommendations and embodied them in its legislation to alter the health service structure in 1990. In doing so it also incorporated a move towards the partial privatisation of all existing local authority services in the area of community care. It aimed to ensure that the relative role of local authorities as the direct providers of care (both in residential homes and community services) would decline in favour of the private sector. Local authorities were to become the 'buyers' of packages of private care for low income people, while their role, as suppliers, of such care declined. There was a great deal of talk about the need for a 'level playing field' on which existing private homes and new private providers of domiciliary care could compete with existing local authority providers. For reasons explored further in the next section, local authorities suspected that they would in practice be 'playing uphill'.

This transfer of responsibility was complicated. It implied mechanisms to shift resources from the social security budget to the local authority social services budget. At a time when the government was already in the middle of dealing with controversial changes in local government finance (see below), it was disinclined to rush this change. It required local authorities to start to plan and reorganise for the new system after the beginning of 1991 but it decided that the scheme should not come into operation in full until April 1993. At the time of writing, arrangements for the transfer remain the subject of complex negotiations between central and local government. The latter fears that it will get insufficient new resources for the job. This fear is reinforced by evidence that the gap is widening between the costs of private residential care and the amount the social security system is prepared to allow residents towards it.

Here again, then, is another social policy measure characteristic of this era, where no new money is being provided but where the structure within which services are to be available is being significantly changed. The extent to which this has wider implications - more privatisation, more handing of costs back to consumers and their families and so on - will only emerge gradually in the course of a long drawn out implementation process.

Central-Local Relations and Local Taxation

In the 1940s Herbert Morrison's bid to put the central welfare state institutions, and particularly the health service, in the control of local government failed. Nevertheless local government already had responsibility for public housing, education and the personal social services (children and welfare services in those days). It was thus responsible for some of the parts of the welfare state which grew steadily, and often without exciting much political controversy through the middle period covered by this book. Central government was gradually imposing more costly duties upon local authorities. Education was particularly significant as a large and growing area of local expenditure. It is the central government which determines most of the duties of local government, enforcing them in the high-cost areas like education and personal social services by inspection systems which take views on the standards of services provided.

Local government expenditure is financed both by local taxation and by grants from central government, so that what local authorities are able to do is quite tightly constrained by statutory controls from the centre. In the early 1960s only around 30 per cent of local expenditure was funded by central government; by 1971 this had grown to 37 per cent and in the 1970s it continued to grow. One political reason for this growth was that the main local source of revenue was the 'rate' imposed upon property, which had to be revised upwards in a very visible way every year in response to the combination of inflation and new demands for expenditure. By contrast the yield of the national income tax rose automatically as incomes rose. Hence rate increases attracted political attention that, in the British unitary state, was as likely to damage central as local politicians. Of course, blaming the centre was in many ways a realistic response by the public in the light of what was pointed out concerning the source of local 'duties'. The central response was to tend to increase the grant.

Once they became engaged in careful central expenditure control exercises, governments of both parties were faced by a problem: that the formulae that had been developed to determine grants to local government (in the pre-computer age) tended to be expenditure-led. Labour, in the 1970s, started efforts to find a new formula for grants which would bring their growth more under control. These efforts were continued resolutely by the Conservatives after 1979 (see Travers, 1986).

This quest was undoubtedly given an added urgency by the fact that one of the responses of the Labour Left to dissatisfaction with the performance of Labour in government was to seek to use local government as a launching pad for socialist advance. An elaborate neo-Marxist debate developed about the feasibility of this strategy; a renewed commitment to local democracy was apparent throughout local government and, in many areas (including in particular London), women and ethnic minorities saw local government as a forum in which to try to enhance their power (see Gyford, 1985; Lansley, Goss and Wolmar, 1989). Despite Conservative Parliamentary dominance in the early 1980s most of the big cities, including London, were ruled by Labour.

Margaret Thatcher saw herself as engaged on a crusade to banish socialism from the land:

> Britain and socialism are not the same thing, and as long as I have health and strength they never will be... (Young, 1989, pp.103-4 quoting a Thatcher speech).

The Labour 'urban socialists' increasingly became one of her targets. She could look out from the Houses of Parliament across the river to where one of the most charismatic of the new Left local Labour leaders, Ken Livingstone, posted London's unemployment figures on the outside walls of County Hall together with, later, defiant political slogans. Hence the quest for new approaches to finding an appropriate modus vivendi for central/local relations - to which the application of the word 'partnership' (Thrasher, 1981) had hitherto not been inappropriate - took on a more confrontational character (Loughlin, 1986).

The Thatcher governments did not find it hard to establish a formula which would determine grants to local authorities which would be independent of their spending patterns. The Department of Environment had the basis for one ready before Labour fell from power. It involved a complex computer model designed to take into account the factors which might affect local needs (see Travers, 1986; Loughlin, 1986). Though too complicated to be carefully examined in political debate, it was capable of manipulation to provide outcomes which steered grants to the kinds of authorities the government wished to favour (in the Conservatives' case, the local governments of the shires and suburban areas where their support lay).

Using this new computer model, central government decided to take its control over local government a stage further. It developed a procedure which deliberately penalised those authorities it deemed to be overspenders. On top of that it did other things. In 1986 it abolished the Metropolitan Counties, all of which were in Labour control and included Ken Livingstone's Greater London Council, and it decided to limit the powers of local authorities to go on increasing local rates. It developed a power which enabled it to 'rate cap' a group of authorities which it deemed to be high spenders.

The government also sought various ways to circumvent local government. A good example of this was the urban programme (see Chapter 5) which by the 1970s had become very much a central/local collaborative venture particularly focused upon employment generation (see Higgins et al., 1983). In the 1980s ad hoc bodies were created (urban development corporations, etc.) to enable central government to intervene directly in urban renewal and 'enterprise zones' were set up where local taxation and planning powers were deliberately weakened. Another example of this circumvention will be found in the following section on education policy.

Once the elaborate structure of controls was set up by the mid-1980s, it might have been thought that central government would leave local government finance alone. However, another problem about local rates was that their level for each household depended upon an archaic valuation procedure. Over time revaluation became necessary. By the mid-1980s revaluation was long overdue in England and Wales. It was carried out in Scotland with results which indicated that there would be a substantial redistribution of the burden of taxation, which would be likely to have an adverse effect upon the already low standing of the Conservatives in Scotland. Thatcher had earlier accepted that, problematical as rates were as a tax, there was no practical alternative. Now she impulsively seized upon a paper by one of the Conservatives' political advisers which suggested that domestic rates could be replaced by a poll tax.

Legislation was prepared (in 1987 in Scotland and 1988 in England) which provided for the replacement of domestic rates by the poll tax or community charge, as it was officially named. In justifying the poll tax the government argued that *all* adults, regardless of householder status and regardless of income (though a rebate scheme provided partial relief for the very poor) should pay for local services and should therefore suffer the consequences of any local extravagance, which could then be 'punished' through the electoral process (Department of the Environment,

Cmnd. 9714, 1986). However, the government had so little confidence in its rationale for the new system that it instituted a mechanism under which high spending authorities were prevented by a capping system from pushing their poll tax levels above a government prescribed ceiling.

At the same time the legislation determined that commercial rates were to have their levels set by central government, thus taking this aspect of local finance out of local government control as well. This had the effect of pushing the share of local expenditure directly determined by the centre up to an average about 75 per cent.

The poll tax was met by a hostile popular reaction which contributed to the end of Margaret Thatcher's career as Prime Minister. After her John Major sharply increased the central government grant to soften the impact of the poll tax, financing this out of an increase in value added tax. He also promised to replace the poll tax by a new tax which would largely reinstate a system of domestic property taxation. His government enacted the introduction of the 'council tax' to begin in April 1993. This involves a simplified form of the former rates, with the number of adult occupants of any domestic property partly taken into account.

Education - Onwards from the Great Debate

The characteristics of Thatcherite education policy clearly relate to the issues discussed above about central/local relations (see Glennerster, Power and Travers, 1991). There are also similarities between the Conservatives' treatment of the health service and their treatment of education, with the difference that education outputs provide (or are believed to provide) an easier basis for evaluation, and therefore for the setting up of competitive relationships between providers, than do health outputs.

The crucial piece of education legislation was the 1988 Education Act, but earlier legislation which extended parental rights to choose schools for their children provided a crucial initial step in what proved to be almost a revolution in British education policy.

The 1988 Education Act largely replaced the 1944 Act as the framework law for state education in England and Wales. This new Act requires that there shall be a 'national curriculum' of 'core' subjects (english, maths and science) and 'foundation subjects' (history, geography, technology, music, art, physical education and another modern language [for over 11s]). There is also a requirement to provide a programme of religious education which reflects the 'dominance' of Christianity in Britain. Curriculum Councils have been set up to keep these developments under review.

The Act also enables the governors of county and voluntary maintained schools, with the support of parents, to apply to the Secretary of State for maintenance by grant from Central Government instead of from education authorities. It also imposes a set of rules relating to the government and management of local authority schools which force local authorities to fund schools on the basis of a centrally determined formula and to delegate significant management responsibilities to governing bodies.

This legislation represents a marked departure from the philosophy of the 1944 Education Act, which left most education under local government control and left issues about the determination of the curriculum largely in the hands of teachers, operating with a eye on the entrance requirements of higher education and the expectations of employers.

In effect, on the one hand, central control over education has been much enhanced while, on the other an attempt is being made to put semi-autonomous schools into a situation in which they are in competition with each other. The theory is that parents make choices of schools by reference to test results. Good schools expand as a result of this and then get more resources. How exactly they expand, when large capital cost issues may need to be overcome, is not so clear. Nor is what is to be done about the declining schools. Improving performance to turn a vicious circle into a virtuous one is easier said than done in a school with under-performing children, falling resources and demoralised teachers.

In any case the issues about the effect of the social catchment area on school performance do not seem to have been addressed in this situation in which the officials of the Department of Education and Science (since spring 1992 called the Department for Education), so long dominant in education (even when Margaret Thatcher was Secretary of State), suddenly seem to have been overwhelmed by politicians determined to make their mark. Parental choice is most likely to be exercised by middle-class parents, thereby enhancing the existing tendency for there to be a hierarchy of schools, influenced by geographical location. Patterns of social and racial segregation may thereby be reinforced. Perhaps more sophisticated interpretation of test results can help ease this problem, a number of academic educationalists seem determined to explore this possibility. Nevertheless old ideas about educational planning, about trying to manipulate catchment areas to create balanced comprehensive schools and about injecting resources to compensate for social disadvantages seem to have been abandoned. Furthermore the combination of allowing choice patterns to determine the social and/or educational character of schools, with testing and the provision which allows some schools to opt out of local authority control (and thereby acquire a measure of control over admittance policy denied to local authority schools) could have the effect of recreating the selective system under-mined by the development of the comprehensive education. Here, then, is another example of the setting up of arrangements for the organisation of policy delivery which may in due course have a fundamental impact upon core aspects of policy itself.

Conclusions and a Postscript

Earlier it was suggested that Margaret Thatcher's impulsive action on poll tax contributed to her fall. That was obviously not the only reason her party moved against her. Increasing divisions on policy towards the European Economic Community, with Thatcher leading from the anti-European wing, also played their part. Overall it was discontent with Margaret Thatcher's leadership style in a quarrelling party, as the next general election approached and Labour seemed at last to be getting its act together which was crucial.

Did Thatcherism fall with Thatcher? Her successor, John Major - very much a Thatcher protege - tried very hard, and presumably with some success, to establish that this was the case in the run-up to the general election. However, there have been no signs of reversals of the policies described above. On the contrary, at the time of writing the establishment of Health Service Trusts and opted-out schools is proceeding, and attempts are being made to find new ways to break up local authority housing departments. Indeed the general assault on local government continues, with expectations that many functions currently run 'in-house' (even things like financial management) will be required to be put out to tender. The ideal for some Conservatives is what has been called 'the enabling' local authority (Ridley, 1988), a small organisation which purchases services for its residents. Major's 'council tax' is a compromise between poll tax and rates.

Major's own contribution to social policy, so far, seems to be the launching of a series of charters for citizens, giving some important attention to service goals but liable to advance further the emphasis upon simple output measures.

Throughout this chapter it has been suggested that the hallmarks of Thatcherite social policy have been a commitment to cost control, not always readily realisable in practice, a readiness to countenance (indeed often welcome) measures which increase inequality, and a zeal for institutional reforms which break up the traditional welfare state bureaucracies (particularly local government).

In the Thatcher era 'high Tory' disdain of detailed concern with the services was abandoned. Margaret Thatcher took a strong interest in social policy.   A number of politicians - Norman Fowler in social security, Kenneth Baker in education, Kenneth Clarke in both health and education - set out to make their names as innovators in social policy. Thatcher's vendetta against local government was enthusiastically carried forward by various ministers, including in particular Nicholas Ridley. John Major has shown no sign of wanting to behave any differently (though he seems likely to proceed more cautiously).

9   Conclusions

Introduction

Welfare states have been compared in terms of their aggregate social expenditures (Wilensky, 1975). Within one state it has therefore been appropriate to look at overall expenditure trends and to consider whether changes in party control or in party policies have had an impact upon social expenditure. This is the simplest of ways of considering the impact of politics upon social policy. The first section of this concluding chapter will therefore review the evidence on expenditure trends, comparing political influences on these trends with other factors.

However, the social programmes of different parties and governments may have different characteristics even if they cannot readily be distinguished in terms of their overall size. A second approach to the question 'what is the impact of politics' involves looking at differences in the way policies have been designed.

A third and final approach involves going beyond simple issues about the design of policy and the impact of party conflict to examine, over the period studied, the nature of the internal politics of social policy. This involves looking at such issues as central/local government relations, relations between politicians and bureaucrats and the role of the politics of the professions. There are questions here about whether the relations between the two government parties and the administrative machine differed, and about whether these relationships changed over time. There are also issues about what was described as 'constituent policy' in the first chapter, policies which have altered the structure of the administration and affected the way policy is implemented.

Explaining Social Expenditure Trends

Throughout the period examined in this book, social expenditure tended to go up in real terms. That increase, as successive chapters showed, tended to accelerate throughout the period 1945 to 1975, though of course there were fluctuations. There were periods when governments temporarily sought to restrain social expenditure - to contribute to the cost of rearming in 1950-51, in the very early years of the Conservative government elected in 1951, and after devaluation by the Labour government in 1968. Conversely there were times, around the 1959 general election and in 1973-75, when social expenditure was allowed to increase very rapidly.

After 1975 the tendency for social expenditure increases to accelerate was stopped, but it continued to grow in real terms. This occurred after 1979 despite a Thatcherite commitment to halt this growth.

By 1990 social security accounted for about 30 per cent of all public expenditure, health and personal social services for nearly another 17 per cent, education for 14 per cent, housing for 3 per cent and employment and training policy for less than 2 per cent. Broadly therefore, social policy expenditure accounted for roughly two-thirds of public expenditure as a whole. The only other big budgets were for defence, accounting for 11 per cent of the total, and law, order and protective services, accounting for nearly 6 per cent.

Rose suggests that:

> Labour favour the Welfare State programmes that collectively account for the largest part of its budget... By contrast, the Conservative Party dislikes high levels of public expenditure on principle... On grounds of party doctrine, whether the Conservative or Labour Party is in office should make big difference to patterns of public expenditure (1984, p.119).

It is difficult to test a hypothesis about the 'effect of party' on the basis of the comparatively few changes of government which have occurred since 1945. The period immediately after the war was an exceptional one, and the third spell of Labour control included the economic crisis of 1975-76. Hence, in many respects the only governments for which even a crude comparison makes much sense are the Labour one of 1964-70 and the Conservative ones on either side of it. Nevertheless, the steady upward trend in expenditure increases across the period 1951-74 does seem to indicate that there will be problems about finding any simple party effect upon expenditure. As suggested in the relevant chapters, there is also little to distinguish the expenditure patterns of Labour post-1975 and the Thatcher governments. Public expenditure increases can be seen as involving a kind of ratchet effect - in which government actions may 'turn the cogs', but they do it alongside other things. Labour's pro-welfare expenditure orientation seems to be but one of the sources of the upward trend.

In another discussion of the same theme Rose has written of 'the inertia of history'. He uses health and social security programmes to illustrate this:

> In 1951 Acts of Parliament authorized twenty-five different programs for a wide range of medical and hospital services and income-maintenance grants to the elderly and needy. Three decades later every one of these programs was still in force, after a series of Conservative and Labour governments had come and gone. Programs enacted before the oldest MP had entered Parliament account for more than three-fifths of total spending on health and social security (Rose, 1989, p.35).

Rose's account makes it sound as if the British system of government is one in which it is constitutionally difficult to repeal legislation. As a system without the checks and balances of federalism or the parliamentary compromises necessary with proportional representation, this it not the case. It is necessary to look for other ways of explaining the continuity.

In various places in the earlier chapters it has been made clear that, in the short run, governments find their expenditure determined by the actions of their predecessors. In 1951 the Conservatives inherited social programmes from Labour whose full expenditure implications were only just beginning to be realised. In the 1970s governments of both political colours found that the public sector incomes policies of their predecessors had substantial implications for them. But in the longer run the room for manoeuvre should have increased. In particular it should have been possible for the Conservatives, who enjoyed two long unbroken spells in office (1951-64 and 1979 onwards), to eliminate programmes involving heavy expenditure commitments they did not like. Certainly, in the case of the Thatcher governments, there have been actions of this kind. Why have they had comparatively little effect?

To answer this kind of question, there is a need to look at the social expectations aroused by the legislation in place, with particular reference to the extent to which these in themselves increase demands upon the public purse.

One important influence upon social expenditure in the period with which this book is concerned is a demographic effect. In terms of need for help from social policy it is possible to identify, in crude age terms, two segments of the population at either end of the age spectrum who may be defined as likely to be 'dependent': those under working age (in somewhat greater need of health services and personal social services early in life and, of course, the main recipients of education expenditure thereafter) and those over working age (recipients of pensions and, with advancing age, increasing users of the health service and personal social services). Some analyses put these two groups together as the 'dependent population'. One such (Halsey, ed., 1988, p.106) adds together, from census data, under 15s and over 65s and shows that they formed 33.1 per cent of the population in 1951, 34.9 per cent in 1961, 37.0 per cent in 1971, and 35.5 per cent in 1981. This suggests that the demographic pressure upon public expenditure was intensifying up to about 1971 but was easing thereafter. However, this data places undue weight upon the impact of the younger end of the age spectrum, where the pressure is primarily upon education and reaches its cost peak around the achievement of adulthood (in fact the heaviest education costs come after the age of 15).

The biggest budget items are health and social security (and within the latter, over half the expenditure is allocated to meet the needs of people over pension age). Hence it is the increase in the size of the elderly group, and particularly the very elderly group, which is of particular importance for social expenditure growth. If attention is paid solely to the older group, the trend is rather different from that described above. The proportions of the population over 65 increased at each census date: from 11.0 per cent in 1951, through 11.9 per cent in 1961 and 13.3 per cent in 1971, to 15.0 per cent in 1981 (ibid.). Finally, it is the old elderly who make exceptionally heavy demands on health and social care systems; people over 80 more than tripled in number and increased from 1 per cent of the population in 1951 to 3 per cent in 1981 (Central Statistical Office, 1992a, p.27).

The establishment of a pensions scheme which seems to make promises of future benefits for its contributors and also creates a general public expectation of support for the elderly, makes it difficult for any government to do other than accept increasing demand and to raise benefits in line with inflation. The establishment of a health service sets up a similar range of expectations of free, or virtually free, health care. Hence, as demographic pressures in Britain contributed to extended waiting lists this became a potent source of pressure upon the government. Opinion data indicate that public support for pensions and health care remained high into the 1980s despite a wider recognition of the case for limits upon social expenditure (Taylor-Gooby, 1985).

A more complicated source of social expenditure increases lies in the fact that, over time, the cost of providing any given service input tends to rise. If that cost rises faster than the rate of inflation, the cost of the service in real terms will increase. The most significant, and controversial, source of such cost increases in the social services is public sector pay increases. Public sector workers expect to enjoy not merely compensation for inflation, but some share in the rising prosperity of the nation. Yet any recognition of the latter in their pay rises produces an increase in public expenditure.

It has been an important feature of New Right beliefs that public sector employees, by virtue of their protection from market forces, are in a position to extract more than their fair share of any increase in general prosperity without making any additional contribution in output such as is required of the private sector (see Heald, 1983, for a good discussion of this complicated subject). Hence the Right-wing attack on those characteristics of the structure of the public services which have been deemed to protect the aspirations of these government bureaucrats (Tullock, 1976), a topic to be examined further below.

But it is not only public sector pay increases which push up the relative cost of public services. Other inputs, such as drugs, may also increase in price faster than the rate of inflation. Furthermore, advances in technology, particularly important in the health care field, increase costs. There is a reasonable public expectation that health care, social care and education will share in the technological advances of the age.

These input cost increases are hard to estimate. Reference was made in Chapters 7 and 8 to some attempts to calculate them, particularly the work of Hills and his colleagues (Hills ed., 1990). Of course, the government expects that improvements in productive efficiency will accompany these increases. These are hard to measure, what is most evident is the rising bill for inputs. Overall, then, the costs of the production of social policy outputs rise over time, accompanying the rise in demand engendered by demographic changes and by technological advances.

Finally, amongst the sources of social expenditure growth which lie outside direct government control, it is important not to forget that benefits and services designed to meet needs and prevent deprivation tend to increase in demand whenever the economy begins to operate less effectively as a source of welfare. This book has not attempted to address this topic in any depth. But some references have been made to the rise in unemployment since 1970, and particularly to its sharp rise in the 1980s. This has not merely increased demand for benefits for unemployed people. It has also increased pressures upon the health system and upon health-related social security benefits. This demand arises not merely because of the direct impact of unemployment on health, but also because partially disabled people are less able to get into the labour market. An economic downturn also increases demands for benefits available to low income workers because it deflates wages and tends to increase the volume of part-time work.

Analyses of the Thatcher era in Britain have shown that, alongside the direct effects of increased unemployment, there have been policies which deliberately increased inequality - in particular shifts of taxation from rich to poor (Hills, 1989) - which again will have had 'knock on' effects upon the demand for social benefits and services. Ironically, inasmuch as the favourite Right-wing device for the rationing of social benefits is the means test, an increase in poverty increases the numbers qualifying for those benefits. The clearest example of this occurs with housing benefit where falling real incomes have pulled an increasing number of local authority tenants into the system. Hence, it is suggested that the attempts to curb social expenditure made by the Thatcher administrations were partly frustrated by an 'own goal' effect arising from their economic and taxation policies.

To sum up this part of the discussion, once a society has a set of welfare policies it has unleashed a series of powerful forces which will tend to maintain and probably increase public expenditure. The creation of expectations of pensions and health care are clearly crucial, particularly in an ageing society, but there are also likely to be rising educational expectations. In addition, there is the fact that social policy has been partly conceived to make a contribution to the protection of individuals from economic misfortune (unemployment and related problems). This also creates expenditure pressures just at those times when economic orthodoxies demand expenditure cut-backs. Taken as a whole these facts are critical for the explanation of the relative absence of a Conservative impact on public expenditure.

In turning to the corresponding failure of Labour to produce expected sharp upward rises in expenditure, it must first be borne in mind, as pointed out above, that the 1945-51 Labour government did preside over a dramatic shift of public expenditure from defence to social policy until 1950. Its panic measures of 1950-51 then threatened to push the pendulum back the other way, though it lost power before this development had lasted long enough to provide a satisfactory test of the impact of the party politics hypothesis. In 1964-70 Labour also significantly increased public expenditure, but the government did not meet the expectations of its supporters, and it has been shown that it did not differ much from its Conservative successor. The latter distinction has perhaps more to do with the erratic behaviour of the Heath government than with the lack of action by Labour. However, inasmuch as there was a 'breach of promise' (Ponting, 1990) by Labour at this time, it had a great deal to do with difficulties in managing the economy and reluctance to shift from the existing consensus over defence policy. Writers like Rose (1989) and Kavanagh (1990) have seen in defence expenditure decline the overall basis for social policy expenditure growth, but it needs to be borne in mind that it was merely a relative and not a significant absolute decline. There was no peace dividend after 1950.

Finally, we reach the 'split' Labour expenditure response in the 1974-79 government, setting off at a fast pace in 1974 and then reining back growth more successfully than any government before or since. Clearly Britain was in exceptional times by then. Labour did not have a clear mandate. The oil price rise was unsettling all economies, but particularly the very vulnerable British one. Electoral studies also show a marked shift of public opinion against public expenditure in this period (Sarlvik and Crewe, 1983). Any political analysis of these events needs to leave behind the simple analysis in terms of ostensible party ideologies and to ask instead, as the quotation from Healey in Chapter 7 suggests, about the bigger political forces in play. These are, of course, the key events for those analyses which talk of a welfare state crisis (for an overall discussion see Mishra, 1984). But crises have to manifest themselves through behaviour. What seems very clear was that at this time leading actors believed that there was a crisis to which they had to respond (see Donnison, 1979, for an analysis of the nature of that crisis, written for a pro-social policy audience).

The most influential version of the crisis theory came from economic analyses which saw public investment as crowding out private investment (Bacon and Eltis, 1976). The Treasury was increasingly of the view that control over the money supply had to be achieved, principally through the control of public borrowing (which meant limiting public expenditure whilst the economy was depressed); indeed Callaghan, the Labour Prime Minister, lectured his own party conference in 1976 that government could no longer spend its way out of a recession. The crucial point, as stressed earlier, is not whether or not there really was an economic crisis or whether the response to it was right or wrong, but that the leading political actors accepted that there was a crisis to which they had to respond in a 'monetarist' way.

Moreover, as Donnison stressed (1979), and Sarlvik and Crewe's evidence seems to confirm (1983), there was a sufficiently large shift of public opinion towards this view to create a considerable problem for the Labour party. In accepting the need for a monetarist response Callaghan widened the split between the Labour government and Labour party (Kavanagh, 1990, Chapter 6) which always tended to emerge as the party faithful saw their ideal goals being disregarded. This split, in which many of the key trade unions supported the anti-government view (particularly the public sector ones), contributed to the conflict during the 'winter of discontent', to losing Labour the election and to producing fierce divisions in the party during the early 1980s. It is clearly the view of analysts of voting behaviour (see Kavanagh, 1990) that Thatcher was able to exploit a populist mood of suspicion about social expenditure, linked to the appeal of promised tax cuts, in a way that was clearly barred to Labour by the commitments of its party members.

This brings us back to other questions about the earlier behaviour of Conservative governments. It has been suggested above that there were strong reasons why Conservative governments might find it difficult to counter the upward trend of public expenditure. However it has been shown that, during the long period of Conservative rule from 1951 to 1964, the economic and demographic upward pressures were not as strong as they were to become. To explain fully Conservative behaviour in this period there is a need to recognise the following:

(1) the ambiguity of Conservative ideology, with a tradition of concern for the preservation of 'one nation' going back at least as far as Disraeli, a 'left wing' which was clearly deeply concerned that there should be no return to the sufferings of the 1930s, and a 'high politics' tradition which was prepared to leave social policy to administrators and professionals;

(2) Conservatives' concern that a belief that Labour would do more for the welfare state would operate to their electoral disadvantage.

It has been suggested above that the mood of the late 1970s enabled the Conservatives to cease to fear the latter, though we still find Margaret Thatcher, in the late 1980s, anxious to assure the electorate that the health service remained safe. It is the changes in Conservative ideology, and the ending of the aloof attitude to social policy which have been particularly important, these which will secure more attention later in this chapter.

Parties, Ideologies and the Design of Policies

The last section has suggested a range of explanations for the absence of a marked divergence between the two major British political parties on social policy expenditure. But simply to look at expenditure patterns is to take a very narrow view of politics. The parties have been shown to appear to differ in their expectations of overall expenditure levels on social policy, but there are other significant ways in which their major policy outputs may be expected to differ. In the absence of a quantitative yardstick, any hypotheses about this are even more difficult to test, but that should not deter this enterprise.

An examination of social policy ideologies suggests that there is likely to be a divergence between the two main parties in their stance on the issue of 'universalism'. The dominant ideology for Labour has been seen to be a 'Fabian socialist' viewpoint (George and Wilding, 1985) which takes as its goal the achievement of services open to all citizens on the basis of need, paid for out of taxation and not rationed by charges. In particular the view has been that means tests should not be used to restrict access to benefits or to determine levels of payment for services, on the grounds that these engender stigma, limit take-up and encourage the development of alternative services for those able to pay for them. A related issue, on which the 'universalists' are not so clear, is whether or not private alternatives should be allowed to exist alongside public ones. From a libertarian perspective there is a reluctance to ban private schools or private medicine, for example. Nevertheless there is a fear that in the absence of active discouragement, some private provisions will be the thin end of a wedge which will undermine universalism. A compromise position on this issue has been a desire to ensure that there are no indirect ways in which the state is subsidising private services (see the 'social divisions of welfare' essay in Titmuss, 1958). It was this concern which led to the examination of the status of private education under the 1964-70 government and to Barbara Castle's efforts to phase out private beds within Health Service hospitals (see Chapter 7).

The main exposition of the universalist approach comes from academic supporters of the Labour party rather than from its political leaders (Titmuss, 1958, 1968; Townsend, 1975). It is recognised that universalism involves many complexities and shades of emphasis (as does the selectivist approach which will be contrasted with it below). What is being emphasised here are particular concerns about methods of delivering public social policies. The main features of universalism, in the view of many Labour activists, have been the following:

- A clear commitment to a free health service throughout the period of this study.

- At the beginning of the period of this study, a strong commitment to the Beveridge scheme, seen as a way to ensure that the sort of means testing associated with the Poor Law could be largely eliminated.

•   Throughout much of the period, an increasingly clear commitment to comprehensive education.

The alternative ideological position to the universalist one has been described as 'selectivism'. The Conservative commitment to this has been less clear than Labour's ostensible commitment to universalism. The clearest expressions of the selectivist viewpoint come in certain New Right articles (Friedman, 1981; Minford, 1984; Harris and Seldon, 1979). In its most complete form the selectivist doctrine involves a view that income deficiencies should be tackled by means of simple means tests, with negative income tax as the ideal approach. Income replacement schemes should put individuals in a position to buy services - health care, social care, education, housing - on the open market. It should not be necessary to provide free services to make up for income deficiencies. There are some problems for this viewpoint about what to do when it is in the public interest that individuals should buy services, but some are unwilling to do so. A particular case arises with education, where parents might refuse to educate their children. A preferred way round this problem advocated by the selectivists is the provision of 'vouchers' which have to be used to 'buy' education.

As has been shown earlier, although this approach has been advocated throughout the period since the *One Nation* pamphlet (Macleod and Maude, 1950), has been quite widely disseminated since the setting up of the Institute for Economic Affairs in 1955 and has attracted considerable attention in recent years, it cannot ever be said to have secured anything approaching complete assimilation into Conservative thinking. Rather it appears as a range of concerns about the targeting of benefits and services, anxieties that some free services may be misused (unnecessary prescribing, for example) and concern to ensure the maintenance of a mixture of public and private systems which provide choices for those able to pay.

However confused party positions may be in practice, there are contrasts in approach which might be expected to manifest themselves in policy decisions over the period studied here.

The universalist approach has, on first sight, come close to being accepted by both parties with regard to health policy. Charges for prescriptions, dental treatment and optical treatment, however, breach that principle. It was shown in Chapter 3 how readily the Labour party began to retreat from the principle of a free service in respect of these items at the end of the 1945-51 period. Clearly the Conservatives were quite comfortable about taking this retreat a stage further. By contrast the 1964-70 Labour government wavered in an unimpressive way on the issue, first abolishing prescription charges and later reinstating them. More recently the Conservatives have been prepared to see charges go up steadily. A difference between the parties with regard to charging was also evident when, in introducing family planning services into the health service in 1974, Barbara Castle over-ruled her Conservative predecessor's decision to impose charges.

The introduction of boarding charges for hospital patients would have made a much bigger inroad into universalism in health care. Macmillan firmly rejected the idea in the 1950s. It has been debated further since but not re-emerged as a serious policy option. However, what has happened during the history of the NHS is that patient stays have been radically shortened, and for many categories of chronically ill or disabled people community care has replaced hospital care. Selectivist principles are applied for all forms of institutional care outside the health service and for most community services.

A comment was made above about Castle's attempt to reduce cross-subsidy from the health service to private medicine. Recent Conservative policies have instead reinforced this and ensured that a thriving private health sector survives alongside the public one.

Overall, therefore, we see Labour's 'universalism' in respect of health care as slightly undermined by its retreat on charges, whereas the Conservative's proclaimed commitment to the National Health Service occurs in the context of the encouragement of a private sector.

It was shown in Chapters 2, 3 and 4 that both parties were proud to claim an adherence to the Beveridge principles, seen initially as solid manifestations of universalism. But it was also pointed out that, in the determination of benefit rates, the 1945-51 Labour government adopted an approach that gave grounds for doubt about the extent to which it could realistically anticipate a minimal role for National Assistance. The actions of the Conservatives between 1951-64 maintained the same situation, so that by the early 1960s it was recognised that the assistance scheme was not in decline. The key to achieving that decline, in the long run, seemed at that stage to lie not in sharp increases in basic insurance benefits but in the addition of earnings-related benefits. Again, both parties agreed on this, differing only in their views about the respective roles of public and private provisions in the pensions field. Not until the Thatcher governments was there a breach in this part of the consensus, when earnings-related short-term benefits were abolished and SERPS was substantially weakened.

But the 1964-70 governments did not only try to improve insurance benefits; they also gave attention to gaps in the coverage of means-tested benefits. In doing so they started a process of elaboration, carried forward much more enthusiastically by the Heath government, which was to start to lead the social security system in a radically different direction. There was clearly a battle going on within the 1964-70 governments between the 'universalists' and politicians like Callaghan who would happily have countenanced the development of Family Income Supplement (FIS) by Labour.

In the 1970s there was then both two more late steps toward universalism by Labour, with child benefit and SERPS, but also the elaboration of means testing by Heath with the introduction of FIS and housing related benefits. Then in the 1980s the Thatcher governments, particularly through the measures introduced in the 1986 Act, pushed the whole system more firmly in the selectivist direction.

In order to carry out a closer examination of the extent to which the Heath and Thatcher governments undermined the Beveridge scheme there is a need to distinguish between the following:

(1) those pieces of the Beveridge design that survived;

(2) those parts of the Beveridge scheme which had collapsed because of weaknesses which had been intensified by social changes, where the Conservatives may be said to have merely given them a 'decent burial';

(3) those parts of the Beveridge scheme which the Conservatives changes did kill; and

(4) social security needs which Beveridge simply did not address, where later innovations need to be assessed in their own right and not by inventing a fictitious Beveridge yardstick.

Flat-rate pensions and benefits for the long-term sick come into category (1). The weakness of the Beveridge scheme was that it set low flat rates and left additions to private provision. In a sense, then, in abolishing earnings-related additions to short-term benefits and in seeking to ensure that many citizens chose private pensions rather than SERPS, the Thatcher governments might have claimed to be 'going back to Beveridge'.

Unemployment benefit comes into category (2). High unemployment produced a situation in which many insurance beneficiaries exhausted insurance entitlements, whilst young people who have never worked have in effect never joined the Beveridge scheme. There are some issues here about the difference between what Beveridge intended and expected as far as unemployment was concerned, and what was enacted (see Chapters 2 and 3).

Also in category (2) is the fact that for many people insurance benefits do not meet their subsistence needs because of the low level at which the Beveridge benefits were set, and because Beveridge did not satisfactorily get to grips with the issues about housing costs. Whether the Conservatives are seen as 'burying' or 'killing' in this case depends upon the view taken about the shift of rent subsidy (on which more will be said below) away from measures to keep rents low to means-tested housing benefits.

The replacement of sickness benefit by employment-based statutory sick pay (for most people) can be seen as the nearest to a direct Conservative assault on the Beveridge scheme, putting it in category (3). But even this is complicated since a residual sick benefit survives for ex-contributors not in employment when they fall sick, and in any case the rebate of contributions to employers in return for payments of sick pay can be seen as delegating responsibility for the benefit to the employer.

Finally, benefits for single parents (other than widows) and additional payments for disabled people are surely in category (4) since they were absent from the final Beveridge proposals. The same can be said about the structure of benefits which supports people in low-paid work, in particular Family Credit and (again) housing benefit.

There have however been areas in which Beveridge scheme entitlements have been weakened, particularly in relation to unemployment. Moreover it could reasonably have been expected that a commitment to the ideals of Beveridge would have involved efforts to improve the scheme over the years, uprating benefits effectively, ensuring that family support (Child Benefit) moved forward with changing times and addressing new issues like family breakdown (which Beveridge did at least discuss). Labour could at least claim that this was its stance (see, for example the quote from the 1964 manifesto at the beginning of Chapter 5). The Conservatives (and particularly the Thatcherite Conservatives) have been only too happy to put means tests at the centre of their approach to social security. In so doing, whilst they have not gone the whole way towards negative income tax, they have damaged the old idea that social insurance involves some sort of 'contract' between state and citizens. The insurance contribution has become merely a tax, not earmarked for social security purposes and certainly not implying irrevocable rights to benefits for contributors. Some of these rights, particularly entitlements to benefits when unemployed, have been quite cynically undermined. There is now no longer even a notional 'insurance fund' to which the government makes contributions to combine with those from employers and employees (see Chapter 3). This was eliminated by one of the Thatcher governments.

There are two levels at which the distinction between universalism and selectivity applied to housing policy. At the first level the system has been socially divided throughout the period covered by this book, and both major parties have accepted and encouraged that. In Chapter 3 Bevan was quoted as believing in a socially diverse public sector, an ideal which does not seem to have been seriously shared by his colleagues. In 1945 there was already a clear social cleavage between owners and renters. As the public sector grew, so did the owner-occupied sector. The latter persistently offered a better bargain, was preferred by better off people and was subsidised through tax relief for buyers. In 1945 about a quarter of households were in owner-occupied dwellings and less than 20 per cent in local authority houses. By 1990 two-thirds of householders were owner-occupiers and most of the rest were renting from either a local authority or a housing association. Until the late 1970s the growth of both owner-occupation and council housing was at the expense of the private sector. Then the sale of council houses began to reduce the size of the latter. Within owner-occupation, there is an inevitable correlation between house quality and economic status.

The other level at which the universalism/selectivity distinction may be applied in relation to housing concerns rent policy within the public sector. Local schemes to adjust rents to incomes date from the pre-war days. The 1964-70 Labour governments actively encouraged local authorities to develop such schemes. The Heath government's Housing Finance Act imposed a national scheme and also extended the principle to the private rented sector. Subsequently housing benefit elaborated this approach. In this respect both parties supported selectivity, but the Conservatives pushed the principle enthusiastically forward. In doing so they moved towards the elimination of subsidies to houses, preferring to subsidise people. Labour opposed the Housing Finance Act's intention to move rapidly in this direction, but decisions taken by the 1974-79 government did not rule this out as an ultimate goal (see Malpass, 1990, for a full analysis of this process). The combination of rent subsidy through social security benefits with the selling of council houses has contributed towards the evolution of the British system towards one in which, as in America, local authority housing is perceived as 'welfare' housing for a low-income population, most of whom are dependent upon social security benefits.

In the middle of the period covered in this book, an examination of the topics of political debate would have suggested that there was a distinct ideological divide between the parties in their approaches to private rented housing. However, in practice, whilst the Conservatives were the initiators of moves towards a free market in rents, they tended to pull Labour reluctantly behind them. 'Fair rents' offered a compromise expression behind which this process could proceed. In the 1980s the Conservatives went beyond this and effectively restored market rents. At the time of writing the erosion of the distinction between the public and the private rented sector is beginning to occur. This involves public sector rents reaching market levels, together with moves which may shift some of it into private hands. Housing benefit is the key device to assist low-income rent payers in all sectors. Labour has opposed many aspects of this evolution; whether the party will reverse it if it gains power remains to be seen.

The last area of policy in which some evidence of a division between the parties can be seen along the universal/selective dimension is education. In this area of policy Labour was the innovator until the 1980s, with the Conservatives opposing the development of comprehensive education quite fiercely when in opposition but accepting it when in power. Perhaps this acquiesence was partly attributable to the preservation of a private sector, containing a little over 5 per cent of the school population, and obviously used by many of the most prosperous families. Opposition to comprehensive education will also have been muted by the extent to which (a) selectivity has been practised within the schools and (b) divisions have emerged within the comprehensive system as a consequence of residential segregation within our society. These two factors are now playing a prominent role in the Conservative backlash against the egalitarianism of the comprehensive revolution, involving the encouragement of developments in the curriculum which enhance divisions within schools, allowing parental choice to operate to extend social segregation and enabling opted out schools to secure some control over their own pupil intakes. Over the period as a whole the Conservatives allowed the universalists to take the initiative, accepting professional domination in education until the 1980s.

Between the four policy areas where there have been divisions between the parties related to differing attitudes to universalism, there are some interesting contrasts. In health and education, universalism moved forward - against a background of the survival of a small private sector.

Labour made the running and the Conservatives, by and large, acquiesced. Even in the Thatcher era the backlash against universalism has been a complex matter, with the government eager to assert, particularly in health, that the 'service' is safe in its hands.

In housing the importance of the owner-occupied sector has meant that universalism has always been fragile. The Conservatives have been the initiators of increases in selectivity, with Labour hostile but at least partly acquiescent. The fact that housing policy has been changed so considerably since Labour was last in power makes it hard to judge where that party really stands on policies concerning this sector.

The last point is also applicable to social security. However, looking back at the 1960s and 1970s, it can be seen that this is an area of policy where Labour - despite some internal divisions, quite a bit of confusion and some problems with the cost of its ideal solutions - tried to move the system forward in a universalist direction. The Conservatives, by contrast, were experimenters with new selectivist policies. The Heath government's introduction of Family Income Supplement and rent rebates were innovations of great importance in the shift towards selectivity which the Thatcher government inevitably continued. Increasingly the system is breaking up into one in which a form of universalism, but with strong encouragement to private pensions, exists for elderly and sick people, whilst selectivity dominates for other groups, in particular the groups like single-parents and low earners to whom the Beveridge scheme offered little.

To sum up the activities of the two main parties in relation to the universalism/selectivity distinction, it can be said that the Conservatives were, until 1979, more comfortable in adopting a pragmatic stance than Labour. Since then their ideologues have argued the selectivist case increasingly effectively, but even in the 1980s governments took steps to distance themselves from its more extreme positions.

Labour, on the other hand, seemed to have embraced universalism enthusiastically and accordingly had to suffer the consequences of disillusion amongst the faithful and divisions within the party when it experienced difficulty in attaining that goal. Some of the least constructive steps taken by Labour governments, in terms of the advancement of social policy, occurred when they were driven reluctantly to make universalist gestures: the abolition and subsequent reimposition of prescription charges; the setting up of the Public Schools Commission which in the end only abolished the hybrid Direct Grant Schools; the immediate repeal of the Housing Finance Act followed by a long dither about what to do next; and the prolonged battle with the doctors over pay-beds when these were only symptoms of deeper problems about the public/private relationship in health.

As suggested at the beginning of this section, one of the problems for universalism lies in the fact that its complete attainment depends upon moves against strong but residual (or by no means residual, in the case of housing) private sectors. One of the underlying problems for Labour about its endorsement of universalism is that it has laid itself open to charges, whether true or not, of being committed to the imposition of uniformity and the prevention of choice. It has been suggested that, in this sense, an initial advantage of being seen as the party of the welfare state became a disadvantage when the above charge was advanced in the 1970s when the public had also come to feel that the welfare state had not lived up to its promise. Clearly this was by no means Labour's only electoral disadvantage in the later part of the period covered by this book. Nevertheless, the earlier acceptance of a bureaucratic delivery system, with professionals dominant in some of the key sectors, was increasingly seen as a problem for the model of social policy delivery championed by the Labour party. Such attacks have come from pro-welfare writers as well as from the New Right. Donnison, for example, points out that the insensitive 'monopolies which impinge most directly on people's lives' in poor areas are state bureaucracies, notably social security offices and housing departments (Donnison, 1991).

Ironically, moreover, where universalism has been the norm, better off and better educated people (loosely, the 'middle classes') have proved themselves more able to make use of the services provided than other citizens (Le Grand, 1982; Goodin and Le Grand, 1987). There was a basis here for a populist innuendo by the Conservatives which portrayed the state-employed middle classes as beneficiaries of the welfare state as both recipients of services and as employees, able to 'exploit' the system alongside poorer 'welfare scroungers'. This provided the opening for an attack upon the policy delivery systems which had been taken largely for granted in the first 30 years of the British welfare state. The next section takes the consideration of this issue further.

The Politics of Policy Delivery Systems, Influencing Policy Implementation

The last two sections have both focused upon party politics. But there are other kinds of politics important for social policy: the politics of the relations between politicians and bureaucrats and the politics of relationships between and within state bureaucracies. Within these categories are the politics of central/local government relations and the politics particularly associated with the efforts of the professions to protect and enhance their power.

It was the arrival of Margaret Thatcher as Prime Minister in 1979 which made a great deal of difference to these aspects of the politics of welfare. The period before 1979 was in various respects one of consensus. The attitudes of the two main parties to the administrative system were broadly the same. The relationship between central and local government was often described as a 'partnership' (Thrasher, 1981) in which governments of one party could work well with local governments of the other, and 'deviant' local councils (like the Labour council at Clay Cross which tried to prevent the implementation of the Housing Finance Act in its area) were disowned by their own national party.

Labour was clearly suspicious of the established civil service (Thomas ed., 1959; Fabian Tract 355, 1964), but its leadership was determined that traditional administrative practices should be respected. In fact it was Heath who moved more effectively than Wilson to try to counterbalance civil service expertise with imported policy advisers.

Professional dominance in the health service was established after a battle in which Bevan was forced to make extensive concessions. A rather quieter, and less greedy, professional dominance in education was accepted by both parties. In the course of the period newer professions grew in strength. Social work secured a surprisingly favourable deal after the Seebohm report, based upon a lack of political interest which allowed policy development to proceed without careful scrutiny. By the end of the period a housing profession was also beginning to establish itself.

Both Heath and Wilson were interested in institutional reform, but this was very much within limits. Local government was restructured without any changes in its functions and without any significant attention to the developing problem of how to finance its activities. The health service was restructured in a way which increased rather than decreased professional dominance. The Fulton proposals for civil service reform were largely ignored, and initiatives like CPRS and the introduction of political advisers had little impact.

In the early period of Margaret Thatcher's rule changes in approach to these issues were slow to develop. The initial changes to central/local relations merely involved the tightening of financial controls, developments very compatible with what had gone before. The government explicitly rejected radical change to the local tax system (Department of the Environment, Cmnd. 9008, 1983). It made changes to the health service largely in order to reduce the complexity introduced by previous reforms (Department of Health and Social Security, 1983). Its approach to the central bureaucracy, apart from public expressions of suspicion about civil service influence which were damaging to morale, was to commit itself to eliminating the corporatist 'quangos' associated, in particular, with the Heath government. This last phenomenon involved a movement in almost the opposite direction to what was to come.

After Thatcher's re-election in 1983 the hunt began in earnest for new curbs upon the power of local government and new ways to run the health and education services. In the central administration the government began to explore ways of creating service delivery organisations separate from the policy-making ministries. At the same time it increasingly took steps to politicise the public service - through attention to whether new appointees to health service bodies, to the new agencies and even to key civil service jobs were people with appropriate 'sympathies' (Young, 1989).

What thus developed was, rather than a direct attack upon welfare services, an assault upon the central bureaucracy, upon professional domination of health and education and upon local government (particularly urban local government which was largely under Labour control). It is suggested that, inasmuch as these were all regarded by the new Tory 'radicals' as bastions of the status quo, they became targets of an indirect attack upon the welfare state. They were the organisations likely to obstruct attacks on welfare; but more significantly they were the organisations whose detailed decisions in the course of implementing policy had a considerable impact upon welfare outputs.

This approach to the politics of welfare clearly owed something to an academic industry which had drawn attention to the difficulty of implementing new policies and to the power of professionals and semi-professionals (Lipsky, 1980; Wilding, 1982). Ironically much of this work had been inspired by a socialist concern about difficulties in adapting policies to the real needs of disadvantaged people. However, there was a related body of work associated with the New Right which portrayed professionals and bureaucrats in the public services as 'monopolists' able to maximise their gains and enlarge their 'bureaus' whilst limiting their outputs (Tullock, 1976). Hence, the creation of diversity and, where possible, competition within the public sector was seen as vital to curb this power. Clearly this relates back to the two earlier themes in this chapter: competition was seen as a way to reduce costs and thus curb public expenditure, and also as a way to increase selectivity (in particular, to provide opportunities for private enterprises to tender for public services). However, it is seen here as a movement in its own right: even where privatisation could not easily be advanced and cost savings were hard to make, the breaking of traditional professional and bureaucratic practices was seen as desirable. The Conservatives had discovered a way to link their other traditional preoccupations to a populist theme - that of opening up welfare state institutions to public control. Increasingly they portrayed recipients of welfare state benefits and services as customers rather than claimants or clients or patients or pupils.

This theme may be linked to the view, increasingly voiced in the 1970s and 1980s, that one of Britain's problems as a society arose from the absence of an enterprise culture. It was shown in Chapter 2 that part of the argument on this attributed this situation to the dominance of the paternalistic elite who were also founders of the welfare state (Barnett, 1986). That elite was also claimed to be dominant in the civil service. Thatcher regarded the civil service as a potential source of obstruction (Young, 1989). Progress of the kind desired by the New Right required not merely replacing people, but also weakening the institutions from which resistance to change might come. However, in the search for explanations of change it is necessary to acknowledge that the causal argument might run the other way. Perhaps, by the 1980s, the traditional elite had been sufficiently weakened by social and educational change for it to be relatively easy for a determined politician to brush them aside. Certainly, the Conservative party itself was much more in the control of 'new' upwardly mobile men and women like Thatcher and Major rather than the old Etonian elite of the Macmillan era.

The chapter on Thatcher's governments commented on her considerable hostility to Labour-dominated urban local government. An important part of this new Conservative approach to institutional reform has had considerable implications for local government. Even though the Conservatives retreated on poll tax once they toppled Margaret Thatcher, their continuing changes in education, housing and community care have further undermined local power. The Conservatives' new populism by passes local authorities, perhaps because 'local socialists' (Gyford, 1985; Lansley, Goss and Wolmar, 1989) had begun to develop an alternative populist movement emphasising responsive and decentralised local government. It involves the development of (a) a direct relationship between locally controlled institutions like schools and central government, (b) consumerist devices which give citizens rights against local government and the latter obligations to make performance data available to citizens, and (c) the concept of the 'enabling authority' buying services from private and voluntary suppliers.

It is not the role of this discussion to assess these developments. They are in any case still very new, indeed still emerging and little researched at the time of writing. There are obviously questions about whether they will deliver what they seem to promise and whether they are perhaps principally the thin end of the wedge of privatisation. They do however have to be recorded as part of a dramatically new approach to policy delivery within the welfare state, weakening traditional provider institutions.

Conclusions

This chapter has examined the events from 1945 to the present day in terms of three approaches to the study of the politics of social policy: one which focuses upon expenditure trends, one which compares competing ideologies and examines how they have actually influenced the policies of governments, and one that goes beyond party politics to look at the politics of the relationships within the system of government.

It suggests that politics has made a difference, but not always in the way that might have been expected from a superficial consideration of political arguments. Its influence on expenditure trends has been complex, since demographic change and economic events have over-ridden political factors. The crucial issues about the politics of expenditure concern the 1975 'watershed' rather than the shifts in party power.

Party politics, however, becomes rather more important when attention is shifted to the universalism/selectivity distinction. However, again there is no simple way of characterising the interaction between the parties. There is rather a complex pattern, varying over time and from policy area to policy area, in which sometimes the universalist tendency in Labour's approach has pulled a pragmatic Conservative party along with it, whilst at other times the power of the selectivist case, in providing choice for those who can afford it and facilitating public expenditure economies, enabled the Conservatives to pull a reluctant Labour party in their direction.

In addition to all this, much detailed decision-making in the welfare state depends upon internal political processes within government as a whole. In relation to this a longstanding consensus about the basic institutional framework has been undermined by the Thatcher governments.

Social policy, when judged in terms of aggregate spending and the range of issues to which the state directs its attention, cannot be said to have undergone a Thatcherite revolution. However, the range of institutional changes of the Thatcher era has been so considerable that it may be right to suggest that there has been some kind of revolution. What is curious about it (making it a revolution in the 'industrial revolution' sense rather than the 'Russian revolution' sense) is that a great deal will depend upon how various implementation processes proceed, and it will be several years (which *may* include a period of Labour government in which it *may* attempt to reverse some policies) before its full effect can be judged.

References

Abel-Smith, B. and Townsend, P. (1955) *New Pensions for the Old*, London: Fabian Tract.

Abel-Smith, B. and Townsend, P. (1965) *The Poor and the Poorest*, London: Bell.

Addison, P. (1975) *The Road to 1945*, London: Cape.

Ascher, K. (1987) *The Politics of Privatisation*, London: Macmillan.

Ashford, D.E. (1986) *The Emergence of the Welfare States*, Oxford: Blackwell.

Audit Commission (1986) *Making a Reality of Community Care*, London: HMSO.

Austin, D.M. (1983) 'The political economy of human services', *Policy and Politics*, **11** (3), pp.343-60.

Bachrach, P. and Baratz, M.S. (1970) *Power and Poverty*, New York: Oxford University Press.

Bacon, R. and Eltis, W. (1976) *Britain's Economic Problem: Too Few Producers*, Macmillan: London.

Bakke, E.W. (1969) *The Mission of Manpower Policy*, Kalamazoo, Michigan: W.E. Upjohn Institute for Employment Research.

Baldwin, P. (1990) *The Politics of Social Solidarity*, Cambridge: Cambridge University Press.

Banting, K.C. (1979) *Poverty, Politics and Policy*, London: Macmillan.

Barnett, C. (1986) *The Audit of War*, London: Macmillan.

Beckerman, W. (ed.) (1972) *The Labour Government's Economic Record: 1964-70*, London: Duckworth.

Benn, C. and Simon, B. (1972) *Half Way There: Report on the British Comprehensive School Reform*, Harmondsworth: Penguin Books.

Berthoud, R. (1985), *The Examination of Social Security*, London: Policy Studies Institute.

Beveridge, W. (1942) *Social Insurance and Allied Services*, Cmd.6404, London: HMSO.

Blackstone, T. and Plowden, W. (1988) *Inside the Think Tank*, London: Heinemann.

Blondel, J. (1963) *Voters, Parties and Leaders*, Harmondsworth: Penguin Books.

Boddy, M. (1980) *The Building Societies*, London: Macmillan.

Bosanquet, N. and Townsend, P. (1980) *Labour and Equality*, London: Heinemann.

Branson, N. (1979) *Poplarism*, London: Lawrence and Wishart.

Brittan, S. (1971) *Steering the Economy*, Harmondsworth: Penguin Books.

Brittan, S. (1977) *The Economic Consequences of Democracy*, London: Temple Smith.

Bull, D. (1980) 'The Anti-Discretion Movement in Britain: Fact or Phantom?', *Journal of Social Welfare Law*.

Butler, D.E. and Rose, R. (1960) *The British General Election of 1959*, London: Macmillan.

Butler, D. and Sloman A. (1980) *British Political Facts 1900-79*, London: Macmillan.

Butler, D. and Stokes, D. (1971) *Political Change in Britain*, Harmondsworth: Penguin Books.

Butler, R.A. in Fowler G. *et al.* (eds.) (1973) *Decision Making in British Education*, London: Heinemann.

Buxton, R. (1970) *Local Government*, Harmondsworth: Penguin Books.

Cairncross, A. (1985) *Years of Recovery: British Economic Policy 1945-51*, London: Methuen.

Castle, B. (1990) *The Castle Diaries 1964-1976*, London: Macmillan.

Castles, F. and McKinlay, R.D. (1979) 'Does Politics Matter? An Analysis of the Public Welfare Commitment in Advanced Democratic States', *European Journal of Political Research*, **7** (2).

CDP (1977) *Gilding the Ghetto*, London: Home Office.

Central Advisory Council for Education (1954) *Early Leaving*, London: HMSO.

Central Advisory Council for Education (1959) *Fifteen to Eighteen* (Crowther Report), London: HMSO.

Central Advisory Council for Education (1963) *Half Our Future* (Newson Report), London: HMSO.

Central Advisory Council for Education (1967) *Children and their Primary Schools*, (Plowden Report) HMSO: London.

Central Statistical Office (1972) *National Income and Expenditure*, London: HMSO.

Central Statistical Office (1992a) *Social Trends 22*, London: HMSO.

Central Statistical Office (1992b) *National Income and Expenditure in the United Kingdom 1990-91*, London: HMSO.

Chapman, R.A. and Greenaway, J.R. (1980) *The Dynamics of Administrative Reform*, London: Croom Helm.

Childs, D. (1986) *Britain since 1945*, London: Routledge.

Cox, C.B. and Boyson, R. (eds.) (1975) *Black Paper 1975*, London:

Dent.

Cox, C.B. and Boyson, R. (eds.) (1977) *Black Paper 1977*, London: Temple Smith.

Cox, C.B. and Dyson, A. (eds.) (1969a) *Fight for Education: A Black Paper*, London: Critical Quarterly Society.

Cox, C.B. and Dyson, A. (eds.) (1969b) *Black Paper Two*, London: Critical Quarterly Society.

Cox, C.B. and Dyson, A. (eds.) (1970) *Black Paper Three*, London: Critical Quarterly Society.

Crosland, C.A.R. (1956) *The Future of Socialism*, London: Cape.

Crossman, R.H.S. (1975, 1976 and 1977) *Diaries of a Cabinet Minister*, (3 volumes.), London: Hamish Hamilton and Jonathan Cape.

Curtis Committee (1946) *Report of the Care of Children Committee*, Cmd.6922, London: HMSO.

Dahl, R.A. (1961) *Who Governs?*, New Haven: Yale University Press.

Dalton, H. (1962) *High Tide and After*, London: Muller.

Davies, J.G. (1974) *The Evangelistic Bureaucrat*, London: Tavistock.

Dawson Report (1920) *Interim Report on the future provision of medical and allied services*, Cmd.693, London: HMSO.

Deacon, A. (1978) 'The Scrounging Controversy', *Social and Economic Administration*, **12** (2).

Deacon, A. and Bradshaw, J. (1983) *Reserved for the Poor*, Oxford: Martin Robertson.

Dell, E. (1991) *A Hard Pounding: Politics and the Economic Crisis*, Oxford: Oxford University Press.

Dennis, N. (1970) *People and Planning*, London: Faber.

Dennis, N. (1972) *Public Participation and Planning Blight*, London: Faber.

Department of Employment (1971a) *People and Jobs*, London: HMSO.

Department of Employment (1971b) *Department of Employment Gazette*, reports in December, p. 1101.

Department of the Environment (1983), *Rates: Proposals for Rate Limitation and Reform of the Rating System*, Cmnd. 9008 London: HMSO.

Department of the Environment (1986), *Paying for Local Government*, London: HMSO.

Department of Health and Social Security (1976) *Priorities for Health and Personal Social Services*, London: HMSO.

Department of Health and Social Security (1977) *Priorities for Health and Personal Social Services: The Way Forward*, London: HMSO.

Department of Health and Social Security (1983) *NHS Management Inquiry* (Griffiths Report), London: HMSO.

Donnison, D.V. (1960) *Housing Policy Since the War*, Occasional Papers on

Social Administration 1, Welwyn: Codicote Press.

Donnison, D.V. (1977) 'Against Discretion', *New Society*, September.

Donnison, D. (1979) 'Social policy since Titmuss', *Journal of Social Policy*, **8** (2).

Donnison, D. (1982) *The Politics of Poverty*, Oxford: Martin Robertson.

Donnison, D. (1991) *A Radical Agenda*, London: Rivers Oram.

Dunleavy, P. (1981) *The Politics of Mass Housing in Britain*, London: Oxford University Press.

Dunleavy, P. and O'Leary, B. (1987) *Theories of the State*, London: Macmillan.

Eckstein, H. (1958) *The English Health Service*, Cambridge Mass.: Harvard University Press.

Eckstein, H. (1960) *Pressure Group Politics*, London: Allen and Unwin.

Ellis, B. (1989) *Pensions in Britain 1955-75*, London: HMSO.

Ely Inquiry (1969) *Report of a Committee of Inquiry into Allegations of Ill-Treatment of Patients and Other Irregularities at the Ely Hospital Cardiff*, Cmnd.3975, London: HMSO.

Enthoven, A.C. (1985) *Reflections on the Management of the NHS*, London: Nuffield Provincial Hospitals Trust.

Esping-Andersen, G. (1990) *The Three Worlds of Welfare Capitalism*, Cambridge: Polity Press.

Evans, P.B., Rueschemeyer, D. and Skocpol, T. (eds.) (1985) *Bringing the State Back In*, Cambridge: Cambridge University Press.

Fabian Tract (1964) *The Administrators*, Tract 355, London: Fabian Society.

Feinstein, C.H. (1972) *National Income, Expenditure and Output of the United Kingdom 1855-1965*, Cambridge: Cambridge University Press.

Field, F. (1972) *One Nation: The Conservatives Record since June 1970*, Poverty pamphlet 12, London: CPAG.

Finch, J. and Groves, D. (eds.) (1983) *A Labour of Love: Women, Work and Caring*, London: Routledge.

Fisher Committee, (1973) *Report of the Committee on Abuse of Social Security Benefits*, Cmnd. 5228, London: HMSO.

Fisher, N. (1973) *Iain Macleod*, London: Andre Deutsch.

Foot, M. (1975) *Aneurin Bevan*, vol. 2, 1945-60, paper edition, London: Granada.

Ford, J. (1969) *Social Class and the Comprehensive School*, London: Routledge and Kegan Paul.

Forrest, R. and Murie, A. (1988) *Selling the Welfare State*, London: Routledge.

Fowler, G. et al. (eds.) (1973) *Decision Making in British Education*, London: Heinemann.

Friedman, M. and Friedman, R. (1981) *Free to Choose*, Harmondsworth:

Penguin Books.

Fulton Committee (1968) *Report of the Committee on the Civil Service*, Cmnd.3638, London: HMSO.

Furniss, N. and Tilton, T. (1979) *The Case for the Welfare State*, Bloomington: Indiana University Press.

Gamble, A. (1988) *The Free Economy and the Strong State*, London: Macmillan.

George, V. and Wilding, P. (1985) *Ideology and Social Welfare*, second edition, London: Routledge.

Gilbert, B.B. (1970) *British Social Policy 1914-39*, London: Batsford.

Glennerster, H., Power, A. and Travers, T. (1991) 'A New Era for Social Policy: A New Enlightenment or a New Leviathan?', *Journal of Social Policy*, **20** (3).

Golding, P. and Middleton, S. (1982) *Images of Welfare*, Oxford: Martin Robertson.

Goodin, R. and Le Grand, J. (eds.) (1987) *Not only the Poor: The Middle Classes and the Welfare State*, London: Allen and Unwin.

Gough, I. (1979) *The Political Economy of the Welfare State*, London: Macmillan.

Gray, A. and Jenkins, W.I. (1985) *Administrative Politics in British Government*, Brighton: Wheatsheaf.

Griffith, J.A.G. (1966) *Central Departments and Local Authorities*, London: Allen and Unwin.

Griffiths Report (1988) *Community Care: Agenda for Action*, London: HMSO.

Guillebaud Report (1956) *Report of the Committee of Enquiry into the Cost of the National Health Service*, Cmd.9663, London: HMSO.

Gyford, J. (1985) *The Politics of Local Socialism*, London: Allen and Unwin.

Halcrow, M. (1989) *Keith Joseph: A Single Mind*, London: Macmillan.

Hall, P. (1976) *Reforming the Welfare*, London: Heinemann.

Hall, P., Land, H., Parker, R. and Webb, A. (1978) *Change, Choice and Conflict in Social Policy*, London: Heinemann.

Halsey, A.H. (ed.) (1988) *British Social Trends since 1900*, second edition, London: Macmillan.

Hambleton, R. (1978) *Policy Planning and Local Government*, London: Hutchinson.

Harris, J. (1977) *William Beveridge: A Biography*, Oxford: Oxford University Press.

Harris, R. and Seldon, A. (1979) *Overruled on Welfare*, London: Institute of Economic Affairs.

Harrison, S. and Wistow, G. (1992) 'The purchaser/provider split in English health care: towards explicit rationing?' *Policy and Politics*, **20** (2).

Heald, D. (1983) *Public Expenditure*, Oxford: Martin Robertson.
Healey, D. (1990) *The Time of My Life*, Harmondsworth: Penguin Books.
Heclo, H.H. (1974) *Modern Social Politics in Britain and Sweden*, New Haven: Yale University Press.
Heclo, H. and Wildavsky A. (1981) *The Private Government of Public Money*, London: Macmillan.
Hennessy, P. (1989) *Whitehall*, London: Secker and Warburg.
Hennessy, P. and Seldon, A. (eds.) (1987) *Ruling Performance: British Governments from Attlee to Thatcher*, Oxford: Blackwell.
Hess, J. (1981) 'The Social Policy of the Attlee Government', in Mommsen, W.J. (ed.) *The Emergence of the Welfare State in Britain and Germany*, Beckenham: Croom Helm.
Higgins, J. (1978) *The Poverty Business*, Oxford: Blackwell.
Higgins, J. et al. (1983) *Government and Urban Poverty*, Oxford: Blackwell.
Hill, M.J. (1974) 'Some Implications of Legal Approaches to Welfare Rights', *British Journal of Social Work*, **4** (2).
Hill, M. (1990) *Social Security Policy in Britain*, Cheltenham: Edward Elgar.
Hill, M. and Bramley G. (1986) *Analysing Social Policy*, Oxford: Blackwell.
Hills, J. (1989) *Changing Tax*, London: CPAG.
Hills, J. (ed.) (1990) *The State of Welfare*, Oxford: Clarendon Press.
HMSO (1944) *Social Insurance: The Government's Policy*, Cmd.6550, London: HMSO.
HMSO (1951) *National Income and Expenditure in the United Kingdom 1946-50*, London: HMSO.
HMSO (1968) *The Administrative Structure of Medical and Related Services in England and Wales*, London: HMSO.
HMSO (1970) *The Future Structure of the National Health Service*, London: HMSO.
HMSO (1972) *Proposals for a Tax-Credits System*, Cmnd.5116, London: HMSO.
HMSO (1977) *Housing Policy: A Consultative Document*, Cmnd.6851, London: HMSO.
HMSO (1989) *Caring for People: Community Care in the Next Decade and Beyond*, Cm 849, London: HMSO.
Horne, A. (1989) *Macmillan*, 2 vols, London: Macmillan.
Howard, A. (1987) *RAB: The Life of R.A. Butler*, London: Cape.
Howe, G. (1965) *In Place of Beveridge*, London: Conservative Political Centre.
Hudson, B. (1992), 'Quasi-markets in health and social care in Britain:

can the public sector respond?' *Policy and Politics*, **20** (2).

Ingleby Committee (1960) *Committee on Children and Young Persons*, Cmnd.1191, London: HMSO.

Joseph, K. and Sumption, J. (1979) *Equality*, London: John Murray.

Kavanagh, D. (1990) *Thatcherism and British Politics*, second edition, Oxford: Oxford University Press.

Kemp, P. and Raynsford, N. (1984) *Housing Benefit: The Evidence*, London: Housing Centre Trust.

Klein, R. (1989) *The Politics of the NHS*, second edition, London: Longman.

Kogan, M. (1971) *The Politics of Education*, Harmondsworth: Penguin Books.

Land, H. and Rose, H. (1985) 'Compulsory altruism for all or an altruistic society for some?' in Bean, P., Ferris, J. and Whynes, D. (eds.) *In Defence of Welfare*, London: Tavistock.

Lansley, S., Goss, S. and Wolmar, C. (1989) *Councils in Conflict: the Rise and Fall of the Municipal Left*, London: Macmillan.

Le Grand, J. (1982) *The Strategy of Equality*, London: Allen and Unwin.

Le Grand, J. (1990) *Quasi-markets and social policy*, Bristol: School for Advanced Urban Studies.

Lindblom, C.E. (1977) *Politics and Markets*, New York: Basic Books.

Lindsey, A. (1962) *Socialised Medicine in England and Wales*, Chapel Hill: University of North Carolina Press.

Lipsky, M. (1980) *Street-Level Bureaucracy*, New York: Russell Sage.

Lister, R. (1975) *Social Security: The Case for Reform*, Poverty Pamphlet 22, London: CPAG.

Lister, R. (1977) *Patching up the Safety Net*, Poverty Pamphlet 31, London: CPAG.

Lister, R. (1979) *The No-cost No-benefit Review*, Poverty Pamphlet 39, London: CPAG.

Lister, R. (1986) 'Burying Beveridge', *Poverty*, **62** (CPAG also published a pamphlet with the same title).

Loughlin, M. (1986) *Local Government in the Modern State*, London: Sweet and Maxwell.

Lowe, R. (1989) 'Resignation at the Treasury: the Social Services Committee and the Failure to Reform the Welfare State', *Journal of Social Policy*, **18** (4).

Lowi, T.A. (1972) 'Four Systems of Policy, Politics and Choice', *Public Administration Review*, **32**.

Macleod, I. and Maude, A. (eds.) (1950) *One Nation: A Tory Approach to Social Problems*, London: Conservative Political Centre.

Malpass, P. (1990) *Reshaping Housing Policy*, London: Routledge.

Marshall, T.H. (1965) *Social Policy*, London, Hutchinson.

McCarthy, M. (1986) *Campaigning for the Poor*, Beckenham, Croom Helm.

McCarthy, M. (ed.) (1989) *The New Politics of Welfare*, London: Macmillan.

Means, R. and Smith, R. (1985) *The Development of Welfare services for elderly people*, Beckenham: Croom Helm.

Merrison Report (1979) *Report of the Royal Commission on the National Health Service*, Cmnd. 7615, London: HMSO.

Mills, C.W. (1956) *The Power Elite*, New York: Oxford University Press.

Minford, P. (1984) *State Expenditure: a study in waste*, Supplement to *Economic Affairs*, 4 (3).

Ministry of Health (1944) *A National Health Service*, Cmd.6502, London: HMSO.

Ministry of Health (1968) *National Health Service: The Administrative Structure of Medical and Related Services in England and Wales*, London: HMSO.

Ministry of Housing and Local Government (various dates) *Housing Returns for England and Wales*, London: HMSO.

Mishra, R. (1984) *The Welfare State in Crisis*, Brighton: Wheatsheaf.

Monckton Enquiry (1945) *Report on the circumstances which led to the boarding out of Denis and Terence O'Neill at Bank Farm, Minsterley, and the steps taken to supervise their welfare*, Cmd. 6636, London: HMSO.

Morgan, A. (1992) *Harold Wilson*, London: Pluto Press.

Morgan, K.O. (1984) *Labour in Power 1945-51*, Oxford: Oxford University Press.

Morgan, K. O. (1990) *The People's Peace: British History 1945-89*, Oxford: Oxford University Press.

Mosca, C. (1939) *The Ruling Class*, trans. H.D. Kahn, London: McGraw Hill.

Mukherjee, S. (1972) *Making Labour Markets Work*, London: PEP.

Murray, C. (1984) *Losing Ground*, New York: Basic Books.

Nordlinger, E.A. (1981) *On the Autonomy of the Democratic State*, Cambridge Mass.: Harvard University Press.

O'Connor, J. (1973) *The Fiscal Crisis of the State*, New York: St Martin's Press.

OECD (1964) *Recommendations of the Council on Manpower Policy as a a Means of Promotion of Economic Growth*, Paris: OECD.

OECD (1970) *Manpower Policy in the United Kingdom*, Paris: OECD.

Offe, C. (1984) *Contradictions of the Welfare State*, London: Hutchinson.

Packman, J. (1975) *The Child's Generation*, Oxford: Blackwell.

Parker, H. (1989) *Instead of the Dole*, London: Routledge.

Pater, J.E. (1981) *The Making of the National Health Service*, London: Kings Fund.

Pelling, H. (1984) *The Labour Governments 1945-51*, London: Macmillan.

Percy Commission (1957) *Report of the Royal Commission on the Law Relating to Mental Illness and Mental Deficiency*, Cmnd.169, London: HMSO.

Phillips Report (1954) *The Economic and Financial Problems of Provision for Old Age*, Cmd.9333, London: HMSO.

Piven, F.F. and Cloward, R.A. (1972) *Regulating the Poor*, London: Tavistock.

Plowden Committee (1961) *Control of Public Expenditure*, Cmnd.1432, London: HMSO.

Ponting, C. (1989) *Breach of Promise: Labour in Power 1964-70*, Harmondsworth: Penguin Books.

Porritt Report, (1962) *A Review of the Medical Services in Great Britain*, London: Social Assay.

Prosser, T. (1981) 'The Politics of Discretion: Aspects of Discretionary Power in the Supplementary Benefits Scheme', in Adler, M. and Asquith, S. *Discretion and Welfare*, London: Heinemann.

Raison, T. (1990) *Tories and the Welfare State*, London: Macmillan.

Redcliffe Maud Report (1969) *Report of the Royal Commission on Local Government in England*, Cmnd.4040, London: HMSO.

Ridley, N. (1988) *The Local Right: Enabling not Providing*, London: Conservative Political Centre.

Robbins Committee (1963) *Higher Education*, Cmnd.2154, London: HMSO.

Robinson, R. and Judge, K. (1988) *Public Expenditure and the NHS: Trends and Prospects*, London: King's Fund Institute.

Rose, E.J.B. et al. (1969) *Colour and Citizenship: A Report on British Race Relations*, London: Oxford University Press.

Rose, R. (1984) *Do Parties Make a Difference*, London: Macmillan.

Rose, R. (1989) *Politics in England*, fifth edition, London: Macmillan.

Rowntree, B.S. (1901) *Poverty: A Study of Town Life*, London: Macmillan.

Rowntree, B.S. (1918) *The Human Needs of Labour*, London: Longmans Green.

Rowntree, B.S. (1937) *The Human Needs of Labour*, London: Longmans Green.

Rowntree, B.S. (1941) *Poverty and Progress*, London: Longmans Green.

Sanderson, M., (1991) 'Social Equality and Industrial Need': A Dilemma of English Education since 1945', in Gourvish, T. and O'Day, A. (eds.) *Britain since 1945*, London: Macmillan.

Sarlvik, B. and Crewe, I. (1983) *Decade of Dealignment*, Cambridge: Cambridge University Press.

Secretary of State for Social Services (1985) *Reform of Social security: Programme for Action*, Cmnd.9691, London: HMSO.

Seebohm Report (1968) *Report of the Committee on Local Authority and Allied Personal Social Services*, Cmnd.3703, London: HMSO.

Seldon, A. (1981) *Churchill's Indian Summer: The Conservative Government 1951-55*, London: Hodder and Stoughton.

Sissons, M. and French, P. (eds.) (1963) *Age of Austerity*, London, Hodder.

Skocpol, T. (1985) 'Bringing the state back in: Strategies of Analysis in Current Research' in Evans, P.B. *et al.* (eds.) *Bringing the State Back In*, Cambridge: Cambridge University Press.

Taylor-Gooby, P.(1985) *Public Opinion, Ideology and State Welfare*, London: Routledge and Kegan Paul.

Thain, C. and Wright, M. (1990) 'Coping with Difficulty: the Treasury and public expenditure, 1976-89', *Policy and Politics*, **18** (1).

Thomas, H. (ed.) (1959) *The Establishment*, London: Blond.

Thrasher, M. (1981) 'The Concept of the Central-Local Partnership: Issues Obscured by Ideas', *Policy and Politics*, **9** (4).

Titmuss, R.M. (1958) *Essays on the Welfare State*, London: Allen and Unwin.

Titmuss, R.M. (1968) *Commitment to Welfare*, London: Allen and Unwin.

Titmuss, R.M. (1971) 'Welfare Rights, Law and Discretion', *Political Quarterly*, **42** (2).

Todd Commission (1968) *Report of the Royal Commission on Medical Education*, Cmnd.3569, London: HMSO.

Townsend, P. (1962) *The Last Refuge*, London: Routledge and Kegan Paul.

Townsend, P. (1975) *Sociology and Social Policy*, London: Allen Lane.

Townsend, P. and Bosanquet, N. (eds.) (1972) *Labour and Inequality*, London: Fabian Society.

Travers, T. (1986) *The Politics of Local Government Finance*, London: Allen and Unwin.

Tullock, G. (1976) *The Vote Motive*, London: Institute of Economic Affairs.

Veit Wilson, J.H. (1992) 'Muddle or mendacity: The Beveridge Committee and the Poverty Line', *Journal of Social Policy*, **21** (3).

Walker, A. (ed.) (1982) *Public Expenditure and Social Policy*, London: Heinemann.

Walker, C. (1983) *Changing Social Policy*, London: Bedford Square Press.

Webb, A. and Wistow, G. (1982) *Whither State Welfare*, London: RIPA.

Webb, A. and Wistow, G. (1986) *Planning, Need and Scarcity*, London: Allen and Unwin.

Wiener, M.J. (1981) *English Culture and the Decline of the Industrial Spirit*, Cambridge: Cambridge University Press.

Wilding, P. (1982) *Professional Power and Social Welfare*, London: Routledge.

Wilensky, H.L. (1975) *The Welfare State and Equality*, Berkeley: University of California Press.

Wilson, H. (1974) *The Labour Government 1964-70*, Harmondsworth: Penguin Books.

Wolfe, A. (1977) *The Limits of Legitimacy*, New York: The Free Press.

Young, H. (1989) *One of Us*, London: Pan.

Young, M. and Wilmot, P. (1957) *Family and Kinship in East London*, London: Routledge.

Index